PREFACE

As one of the five career manuals in the *Basic Spanish Grammar,* Fourth Edition, program, *Spanish for Teachers,* Fourth Edition, presents the specialized vocabulary that is needed by teachers of Spanish-speaking elementary- and secondary-school students. *Spanish for Teachers* also provides opportunities to apply, in a wide variety of practical contexts, the grammatical structures introduced in the corresponding lessons of the *Basic Spanish Grammar* core text.

Features of the New Edition

- Each of the twenty lessons of *Spanish for Teachers* focuses on a common school situation, such as a math lesson, recess activities, or a parent-teacher conference.
- Realistic dialogues model typical conversations and present the words and expressions that teachers need in the classroom and around the school. Vocabulary is supplied for teaching basic subjects such as English, science, history, and math.
- A revised grammatical sequence now provides earlier practice of the familiar (*tú*) command, which is introduced in Lesson 11 of *Basic Spanish Grammar.*
- The end-of-lesson vocabulary expansion sections teach additional terms that are useful for communicating in the situations presented in the lessons.
- A vocabulary review after every five lessons helps students check their understanding of key words and phrases.
- The Appendix has been expanded and revised to include a tapescript for "Introduction to Spanish Sounds" (on cassette), so students can more readily study Spanish pronunciation.
- The audiocassette program for *Spanish for Teachers* has been revised in accordance with changes made in the lessons.
- A sample vocabulary quiz and two final exams for *Spanish for Teachers* are available in a separate booklet that also includes the testing program for the *Basic Spanish Grammar* core text.
- The new Instructor's Edition of *Basic Spanish Grammar* offers suggestions for organizing, testing, and grading classes for career-oriented students.

Organization of the Lessons

- A Spanish dialogue introduces key vocabulary and grammatical structures in the context of a particular teaching situation. Since this manual is intended for teachers at a variety of grade levels, the purpose of the dialogues is to present as much vocabulary as possible related to a given topic, rather than to demonstrate an actual teaching module. Therefore, concepts that actually would be taught at different grade levels may appear in the same dialogue.
- The English translation of the dialogue follows the Spanish version so students can quickly check their understanding of specific words and phrases.
- A new vocabulary list summarizes words and phrases introduced in the dialogue and categorizes them by part of speech. Cognates are presented in a special section so that students can easily identify and use these terms.
- A multistep practice section provides opportunities for students to use new vocabulary and grammar in the context of the lesson theme and includes the following types of activities:
  —Structural exercises that provide practice of important grammar points using the new vocabulary.
  —Question-answer exercises that check comprehension of the dialogue and also elicit personal, topically-related ideas and experiences.
  —Dialogue completion exercises that encourage students to apply their own experiences and imaginations while practicing new vocabulary and grammar.
  —Situational exercises that explore what one might say in specific circumstances related to the theme of the lesson. For example, Lesson 15 (*En la clase de ciencias*) poses situations in which a teacher must explain to a student some basic concepts of astronomy, physics, and chemistry.

—Open-ended "You're on your own!" roleplays that present opportunities for pairs of students to enact situations similar to those they might encounter in their work as teachers.

- Each lesson concludes with an optional vocabulary expansion section focusing on additional words and phrases that are useful in the context of the lessons. For example, Lesson 5, which is about an art class, includes terms for art supplies and prepositions of location (on top of, behind, etc.). A practice exercise accompanies each vocabulary expansion section.

Vocabulary Review Sections

A vocabulary review section appears after every five lessons to allow students to check their progress. Each review section contains four exercises, including matching, sentence completion, and crossword puzzles. Crossword puzzle solutions appear in Appendix C.

Appendixes

- Appendix A, "Introduction to Spanish Sounds," is the tapescript for the opening pronunciation section on the accompanying audiocassette program. It briefly explains each Spanish vowel and consonant sound and the concept of linking. Examples and practice are included.
- Appendix B, "Spanish Pronunciation," offers a more detailed exploration of Spanish sounds, outlining the basic rules and principles governing pronunciation, with helpful suggestions for improving pronunciation.
- Appendix C, "Answer Key to the *Crucigramas*," supplies the solutions to the crossword puzzles found in the vocabulary review sections.
- The comprehensive Spanish-English/English-Spanish Vocabulary includes all the words and expressions introduced in the twenty lessons.

Audiocassette Program

Spanish for Teachers, Fourth Edition is accompanied by a complete audiocassette program containing "Introduction to Spanish Sounds" (Appendix A), followed by the dialogue and the vocabulary list for each lesson.

A FINAL WORD

The many students who have used *Spanish for Teachers* in previous editions have enjoyed learning and practicing their new language in realistic contexts. We hope that the Fourth Edition will prepare today's students to better communicate with the Spanish-speaking pupils and parents whom they encounter in their work as teachers.

We would like to hear your comments on and reactions to *Spanish for Teachers* and to the *Basic Spanish Grammar* program in general. Reports of your experiences using this program would be of great interest and value to us. Please write to us care of D. C. Heath and Company, Modern Languages, College Division, 125 Spring Street, Lexington, Massachusetts 02173.

Acknowledgments

We wish to thank our colleagues who have used previous editions of *Spanish for Teachers* for their constructive comments and suggestions.

We also wish to express our gratitude to the editorial and production staff of D. C. Heath and Company. José Blanco, Nicole Cormen, Katherine McCann, Gina Russo, and Denise St. Jean provided us with assistance and encouragement during the preparation of the manuscript.

Ana C. Jarvis

Raquel Lebredo

Spanish for Teachers

Third Edition

Ana C. Jarvis
Chandler-Gilbert Community College

Raquel Lebredo
California Baptist College

D. C. Heath and Company
Lexington, Massachusetts   Toronto

Cover: We Know They Made Pottery and Lived in Elaborately Decorated Rooms, 48″ × 55″, watercolor, © 1988, by Lisa Houck.

International Standard Book Number: 0–669–24305–1

Preliminary Lesson 1

En el aula
(*In the classroom*)

These are the names of the people and the things one sees in a classroom. Learn to say them in Spanish.

Let's see how much you remember!

Review the words referring to people and objects you see in the classroom and then name the following:

1. ....

2. ....

3. ....

4. ....

5. ....

6. ....

7. ....

8. ....

9. ....

10. ....

11. ....

12. ....

13. ....

14. ....

15. ....

16. ....

17. ....

Preliminary Lesson 2

Algunas expresiones útiles
(*Some useful expressions*)

When Speaking to One Child	When Speaking to the Whole Class	English Equivalent
1. Abre (Cierra) tus libros.	Abran (Cierren) sus libros.	Open (Close) your books.
2. Escribe.	Escriban.	Write.
3. Escucha.	Escuchen.	Listen.
4. Estudia la lección __ .	Estudien la lección __ .	Study lesson __ .
5. Siéntate.	Siéntense.	Sit down.
6. Ve a la página __ .	Vayan a la página __ .	Go to page __ .
7. Entrega la tarea (los exámenes).	Entreguen la tarea (los exámenes).	Turn in your homework (the exams).
8. Presta atención.	Presten atención.	Pay attention.
9. Cállate,	Cállense.	Be quiet.
10. Ve a la pizarra.	Vayan a la pizarra.	Go to the board.
11. No corras.	No corran.	Don't run.
12. No empujes.	No empujen.	Don't push.
13. Levanta la mano.	Levanten la mano.	Raise your hand(s).
14. Vuelve a tu asiento.	Vuelvan a sus asientos.	Go back to your seat(s).

Otras palabras útiles
    (Other useful words)

1. Dictado   Dictation
2. Presente   Present, Here
3. Ausente   Absent

LET'S SEE HOW MUCH YOU REMEMBER!

Match the items in column A with the items in column B.

A	*B*
1. Escriban. ____	1. Sit down.
2. Ve a la pizarra. ____	2. Don't run.
3. Vayan a la página· ____	3. Listen.
4. Entreguen la tarea. ____	4. Go back to your seats.
5. Presten atención. ____	5. Write.
6. Escucha ____	6. Open your books.
7. Levanta la mano. ____	7. Don't push.
8. No corras. ____	8. Go to the board.
9. Estudien la lección ____ .	9. Study the lesson.
10. Siéntense. ____	10. Go to page ____.
11. Cállense. ____	11. Turn in your homework.
12. No empujes. ____	12. Dictation.
13. Vuelve a tu asiento. ____	13. Absent.
14. Presente. ____	14. Pay attention.
15. Dictado. ____	15. Here.
16. Ausente. ____	16. Be quiet.
17. Abran sus libros. ____	17. Raise your hand.

Lesson 1

Conversaciones con la maestra

La maestra habla con la[1] señora Vera.

MAESTRA —María necesita mejorar, señora Vera.
SRA. VERA —No trabaja mucho, ¿verdad?
MAESTRA —No, y siempre habla en clase.
SRA. VERA —¿Participa en clase?
MAESTRA —Muy poco. Y no presta atención.
SRA. VERA —¿Qué necesita repasar?
MAESTRA —La tabla de multiplicar. También necesita leer más.
SRA. VERA —Siempre lleva tarea a casa.
MAESTRA —¡Porque nunca termina el trabajo aquí!
SRA. VERA —Bueno… la niña necesita ayuda.

La maestra habla con el[1] señor Alba.

SR. ALBA —¿Algún problema con Pepito?
MAESTRA —¡No! Pepito trabaja muy bien. Ya suma, resta, y multiplica.
SR. ALBA —¿Y en lectura?
MAESTRA —Bueno… a veces no escucha las instrucciones.
SR. ALBA —Pepito trabaja mejor independientemente.
MAESTRA —Sí, pero a veces necesita trabajar con los demás.
SR. ALBA —Sí. ¡Ah! ¿Qué significa la *O* en la libreta de calificaciones?
MAESTRA —La *O* significa "sobresaliente", la *S*, "satisfactorio" y la *N*, "necesita mejorar".
SR. ALBA —Muy bien. Gracias. ¿Dónde firmo?
MAESTRA —Aquí, por favor.

*   *   *

Conversations with the Teacher

The teacher speaks with Mrs. Vera.

TEACHER: Mary needs to improve, Mrs. Vera.
MRS. VERA: She doesn't work much, right?
TEACHER: No, and she always talks in class.
MRS. VERA: Does she participate in class?
TEACHER: Very little. And she doesn't pay attention.
MRS. VERA: What does she need to review?
TEACHER: The multiplication table. She also needs to read more.
MRS. VERA: She always takes homework home.
TEACHER: Because she never finishes the work here!
MRS. VERA: Well . . . the child needs help.

---

[1]When referring to a third person and using a title, the definite article is used.

The teacher speaks with Mr. Alba.

MR. ALBA: Any problem with Pepito?
TEACHER: No! Pepito works very well. He already adds, subtracts, and multiplies.
MR. ALBA: And in reading?
TEACHER: Well . . . sometimes he doesn't listen to the instructions.
MR. ALBA: Pepito works better independently.
TEACHER: Yes, but sometimes he needs to work with the others.
MR. ALBA: Yes. Ah! What does the *O* mean in the report card?
TEACHER: The *O* means "outstanding", the *S,* "satisfactory," and the *N,* "needs to improve."
MR. ALBA: Very well. Thank you. Where do I sign?
TEACHER: Here, please.

VOCABULARY

COGNATES

la **atención** attention	la **instrucción** instruction
la **conversación** conversation	**mucho,(-a)** much
independientemente independently	**satisfactorio,(-a)** satisfactory

NOUNS

la **ayuda**   help
la **lectura**   reading
la **libreta de calificaciones**   report card
la **niña**   girl, child (female)
la **tarea**   homework
el **trabajo**   work

VERBS

escuchar   to listen
firmar   to sign
llevar   to take, to carry
mejorar   to improve
multiplicar   to multiply
participar   to participate
repasar   to review
restar   to subtract
significar   to mean, to stand for, to signify
sumar   to add, to add up
terminar   to finish

ADJECTIVES

sobresaliente   outstanding

OTHER WORDS AND EXPRESSIONS

a casa   home
a veces   sometimes
algún   any
aquí   here
bueno...   well . . .
con   with
¿dónde?   where?
en clase   in class
leer más   to read more
los demás   the others
mejor   better
muy bien   very well
muy poco   very little
nunca   never
pero   but
porque   because
prestar atención   to pay attention
¿qué?   what?
¿qué significa...?   what does . . . mean?
siempre   always
tabla de multiplicar   multiplication table
también   also
¿verdad?   right?, true?
ya   already

LET'S PRACTICE!

Rewrite the following, using the new subject.   Make all necessary changes.

1. ¿Roberto ya suma, resta y multiplica?

   ¿Ellos .... ?

2

2. ¿Dónde firmo?

¿ .... usted?

3. Ella lleva tarea a casa porque no termina el trabajo aquí.

Nosotros ....

4. Juan habla mucho en clase y no presta atención.

Tú ....

5. No mejoramos porque no repasamos las lecciones.

La niña ....

6. Tú no escuchas las instrucciones y no participas en clase.

Yo ....

CONVERSATION

Answer the following questions based on the dialogue.

1. ¿Qué necesita María?

    ....

2. ¿Participa María en clase?

    ....

3. ¿Qué necesita repasar la niña?

    ....

4. ¿Necesita María leer más también?

    ....

5. ¿Lleva María tarea a casa?

    ....

6. ¿Termina María el trabajo en clase?

    ....

7. ¿Necesita ayuda María?

    ....

8. ¿Trabaja bien Pepito?

    ....

9. ¿Escucha Pepito las instrucciones?

   ....

10. ¿Trabaja Pepito mejor con los demás?

   ....

11. ¿Qué significa la *N* en la libreta de calificaciones?

   ....

Some additional questions.

12. ¿Trabaja Ud. mucho?

   ....

13. ¿Participan Uds. en clase?

   ....

14. ¿Necesita Ud. mejorar en español?

   ....

15. ¿Trabaja Ud. mejor independientemente o con los demás?

   ....

16. ¿Necesitan Uds. ayuda?

   ....

DIALOGUE COMPLETION

Using your imagination and the vocabulary learned in this lesson, complete the missing lines of this dialogue.

Una conversación.

SRA. ALBO   —...

MAESTRA   —No señora, la niña nunca termina la tarea.

SRA. ALBO   —...

MAESTRA   —Sí, señora, habla mucho en clase.

SRA. ALBO   —...

MAESTRA   —No, no participa mucho en clase y no presta atención.

SRA. ALBO   —...

MAESTRA   —Sí, señora, suma y resta bien, pero no multiplica bien.

SRA. ALBO   —...

MAESTRA   —Lleva tarea a la casa porque no termina el trabajo aquí.

SRA. ALBO   —...

MAESTRA   —Sí, trabaja bien con los demás, pero a veces no escucha las instrucciones.

SRA. ALBO   —...

MAESTRA   —Sí, la niña necesita mucha ayuda.

SRA. ALBO   —...

MAESTRA   —Sí, también necesita mejorar en lectura.

SRA. ALBO   —...

MAESTRA   —Aquí, por favor.

SRA. ALBO   —...

MAESTRA   —De nada.

SITUATIONAL EXERCISES

What would you say in the following situations?

1. You are talking to a parent. Tell him his son does not participate in class, and does not pay attention. Tell him also that he needs to review the multiplication table.
2. You are a parent. Ask your child's teacher if your child needs help. Tell her your child always takes homework home. Ask her if he/she does not finish the work in class.
3. You are explaining the grading system to a parent. Tell him/her what *O*, *S*, and *N* stand for.
4. You are a parent. Tell your child's teacher that your child works better with (the) others, but he does not work very well independently.
5. You are talking with your child's teacher. Ask him/her if (there is) any problem with the child. Ask him/her if he needs to improve.

YOU'RE ON YOUR OWN!

With a classmate, act out the following situations:

1. A teacher having a conference with the parent of a very good student.
2. A teacher having a conference with the parent of a very poor student.

VOCABULARY EXPANSION (Optional)

Useful vocabulary when writing a report card:

Lectura	Reading
comprensión	comprehension
lectura oral	oral reading
sonidos	sounds

Aritmética, Matemáticas	Arithmetic, Math
sumas	additions
restas	subtractiones
multiplicaciones	multiplications
divisiones	divisions
cuentas	math problems

Lenguaje	Language
ortografía	spelling

Ciencias Sociales	Social Science
Arte	Art
Música	Music
Educación Física	Physical Education
Esfuerzo	Effort
Conducta	Citizenship

Do you remember the words used in the Vocabulary Expansion?

Give the Spanish equivalent of the following words.

arithmetic problems ....

subtraction ....

vocabulary ....

social science ....

reading ....

citizenship ....

addition ....

comprehension ....

spelling ....

physical education ....

art ....

music ....

multiplication ....

effort ....

division ....

math

Lesson 2

En la escuela

La señorita Soto habla con los niños en la clase. Primero pasa lista.

SRTA. SOTO	—Buenos días, niños. ¿Cómo están?
NIÑOS	—Buenos días, señorita.
SRTA. SOTO	—(*Pasa lista*) José Jiménez.
JOSÉ	—Presente.
SRTA. SOTO	—Ana Rodríguez.
CARLOS	—Ausente…

(*Después de pasar lista*)

SRTA. SOTO	—(a Carlos) ¿Necesitas lápiz y papel?
CARLOS	—No, señorita, pero necesito una pluma y el libro de lectura.[1]
SRTA. SOTO	—Siempre debes traer el libro de lectura a la escuela, Carlos.
MARÍA	—Señorita, ¿escribo la fecha en la pizarra?
SRTA. SOTO	—Sí, María. Raúl, ¿qué fecha es hoy?
RAÚL	—Hoy es el veinticinco de septiembre, señorita.
LUPE	—¿Qué páginas leemos hoy, señorita?
SRTA. SOTO	—Hoy deben leer las páginas trece, catorce y quince.
LUPE	—¿Leemos en voz alta?
SRTA. SOTO	—No, con la vista… ¡Silencio, niños!

Después de la hora de lectura los niños trabajan en grupos.

JULIÁN	—Señorita, Alicia y yo necesitamos lápices rojos, azules y amarillos.
SRTA. SOTO	—Muy bien. Deben colorear los rectángulos con azul, los círculos con anaranjado, los cuadrados con rosado y los triángulos con marrón.
JULIÁN	—¿Abro la ventana, señorita?
SRTA. SOTO	—Sí, por favor.
CARMEN	—Necesito ir al baño, señorita.
SRTA. SOTO	—Debes esperar un momento, Carmen.
ROSA	—¿Borro las palabras de la pizarra, señorita?
SRTA. SOTO	—No, todavía no. Todos deben copiar el vocabulario en el cuaderno de ejercicios.

(*Entra la secretaria*)

SECRETARIA	—Señorita Soto, llaman a José Jiménez por teléfono.
SRTA. SOTO	—Gracias. (*A los niños*) ¡Es la hora del recreo! ¡Ah! ¿Quiénes comen hoy en la cafetería? Levanten la mano.

---

[1]Spanish uses prepositional phrases that correspond to the English adjectival use of nouns *reading book—libro de lectura.*

7

At School

Miss Soto speaks with the children in the classroom.   First she calls the roll.

MISS SOTO:	Good-morning, children. How are you?
CHILDREN:	Good-morning, teacher (miss).
MISS SOTO:	(*calls the roll*) Jose Jimenez.
JOSE:	Here!
MISS SOTO:	Ana Rodriguez.
CARLOS:	Absent.

(*After calling the roll*)

MISS SOTO:	(*to Carlos*) Do you need a pencil and paper?
CARLOS:	No, teacher (miss), but I need (a) pen and the reading book.
MISS SOTO:	You must always bring the reading book to school, Carlos.
MARIA:	Teacher (miss), shall I write the date on the board?
MISS SOTO:	Yes, Maria. Raul, what's the date today?
RAUL:	Today is September 25th, Miss.
LUPE:	What pages do we read today, teacher, (miss)?
MISS SOTO:	Today you must read pages 13, 14, and 15.
LUPE:	Shall we read aloud?
MISS SOTO:	No, silently . . . Silence, children!

After reading time the children work in groups.

JULIAN:	Teacher, Alice and I need red, blue and yellow pencils.
MISS SOTO:	Very well. You must color the rectangles (with) blue, the circles (with) orange, the squares (with) pink, and the triangles (with) brown.
JULIAN:	Shall I open the window, Miss?
MISS SOTO:	Yes, please.
CARMEN:	I need to go to the bathroom, teacher.
MISS SOTO:	You must wait a moment, Carmen.
ROSA:	Shall I erase the words on the board, teacher (miss)?
MISS SOTO:	No, not yet. Everybody must copy the vocabulary in the workbook.

(*The secretary comes in.*)

SECRETARY:	Miss Soto, they want Jose Jimenez on the phone.
MISS SOTO:	Thank you. (*To the children*) It's recess time. Ah!, who is eating in the cafeteria today? Raise your hands!

VOCABULARY

COGNATES

la **cafetería** cafeteria	el **rectángulo** rectangle
la **clase** class	el, la **secretario(-a)** secretary
el **grupo** group	el **silencio** silence
la **lista** list, roll	el **triángulo** triangle
presente present	el **vocabulario** vocabulary

NOUNS

el **baño** bathroom	la **escuela** school
el **círculo** circle	la **fecha** date
el **cuadrado** square	la **hora** hour
el **ejercicio** exercise	el **niño** boy, child

los, las **niños(-as)** children
la **página** page
la **palabra** word
el **papel** paper

VERBS

borrar to erase
colorear to color
copiar to copy
deber must, should
llamar to call
traer[1] to bring

ADJECTIVES

amarillo(-a) yellow
anaranjado(-a) orange
azul blue
marrón, café brown
rojo(-a) red
rosado(-a) pink

OTHER WORDS AND EXPRESSIONS

a la escuela to school

¿cómo están? How are you? (when talking to more than one person)
con la vista, en silencio silently, silent (reading)
cuaderno de ejercicios workbook
después (de) after
en on
en voz alta aloud
en la escuela at school
es la hora del recreo (receso) it is recess time
hora de lectura reading time
hoy today
ir al baño to go to the bathroom
levanten la mano raise your hands
libro de lectura reading book
llamar por teléfono to call on the phone
pasar lista to call roll
primero(-a) first
quienes who (plural)
todavía no not yet
todos(-as) all, everybody
un momento one moment

LET'S PRACTICE!

Rewrite the following sentences, according to the new elements. Make all the necessary changes.

1. Necesito un lápiz rojo. (plumas)

   ....

2. Ella debe traer los libros a la escuela. (Nosotros)

   ....

3. Necesito el libro azul. (azules)

   ....

4. Colorea el círculo con el lápiz amarillo. (tizas)

   ....

5. Escriben en el cuaderno de ejercicios. (el pizarrón)

   ....

6. ¿Los niños leen la página quince? (Tú)

   ....

---

[1]This verb is not regular, and will be conjugated later.

CONVERSATION

Answer the following questions based on the dialogue:

1. ¿Con quién habla la señorita Soto?

   ....

2. ¿Pasa lista la señorita Soto?

   ....

3. ¿Qué necesita Carlos?

   ....

4. ¿Quién escribe la fecha en la pizarra?

   ....

5. ¿Qué páginas deben leer los niños?

   ....

6. ¿Deben los niños leer en voz alta?

   ....

7. ¿Con qué color deben los niños colorear los rectángulos? (¿los triángulos?)

   ....

8. ¿Desea Julián abrir la ventana?

   ....

9. ¿Qué necesita Carmen?

   ....

10. ¿Dónde deben copiar los niños el vocabulario?

    ....

11. ¿Quién entra en la clase?

    ....

12. ¿A quién llaman por teléfono?

    ....

Some additional questions:

13. ¿Necesita Ud. el lápiz o la pluma?

    ....

14. ¿Qué fecha es hoy?

....

15. ¿Pasa Ud. siempre lista?

....

16. ¿Lee Ud. en voz alta o con la vista?

....

17. ¿Copia Ud. el vocabulario en el cuaderno de ejercicios?

....

18. ¿Come Ud. hoy en la cafetería?

....

DIALOGUE COMPLETION

Using your imagination and the vocabulary learned in this lesson, complete the missing lines of this dialogue.

La maestra habla con Rosita:

MAESTRA —Rosita, es la ahora de lectura.

ROSITA —...

MAESTRA —¿Necesitas el libro de lectura? Pero, Rosita, siempre debes traer el libro a clase.

ROSITA —...

MAESTRA —Primero debes leer la página 15 y después la página 16.

ROSITA —...

MAESTRA —No. Debes leer en voz alta.

CARLOS —...

MAESTRA —No, todavía no debes borrar la pizarra. Debes esperar un momento.

CARLOS —...

MAESTRA —Sí, necesitas repasar el vocabulario después de la hora de recreo.

CARLOS —...

MAESTRA —Hoy es el 10 de mayo. (a todos los niños) ¿Quiénes necesitan ir al baño? Levanten la mano.

SITUATIONAL EXERCISES

What would you say in the following situations?

1. Greet your students and ask them how they are.
2. Tell your students that they must write the date in their (the) notebook. Tell them today is May second.
3. You are talking to your Spanish teacher. Ask him what pages you should study. Ask him also if you should read aloud.
4. Ask one of your students if he needs to go to the bathroom. Ask the rest of the class who's eating in the cafeteria. Tell them to raise their hands.
5. Tell your students to color the squares brown, the circles blue, the triangles orange, and the rectangles pink.
6. Your students are being very noisy. After telling them to be quiet, tell them everyone must copy the vocabulary in the workbook.
7. You are in your Spanish class. The teacher calls your name. Answer. The teacher then calls the name of a student who is not there. Answer for him. Then tell your teacher you need (a) pen and (some) paper.
8. One of your students always forgets his reading book. Talk to him.
9. Ask your teacher if you should erase the words on the board.
10. Tell your teacher that they want Maria Vera on the phone.

YOU'RE ON YOUR OWN!

With a classmate, act out the following:

A teacher and her students (one partner will play the role of several children)

VOCABULARY EXPANSION (Optional)

A. Terms that refer to color or coloring:

1. **morado(-a)** purple
2. **gris** gray
3. **claro(-a)** light
4. **oscuro(-a)** dark
5. **sombrear** to shade

B. Interrogative words:

1. **cuándo** when
2. **cómo** how
3. **quién(-es)** who
4. **por qué** why
5. **cuántos(as)** how many
6. **qué** what
7. **dónde** where

C. Other people who work at a school:

1. **el(la) director(-a)** principal
2. **el(la) vicedirector(-a)** vice principal
3. **el(la) enfermero(-a)** nurse

Do you remember the words used in the Vocabulary Expansion?

A. Write the questions that originated the following answers:

1. *Bien*, gracias. ¿Y usted?

....

2. Los niños estudian ciencias sociales *los lunes*.

   ....

3. Los niños comen *en la cafetería*.

   ....

4. *Irma* borra la pizarra.

   ....

5. Deben colorear *los cuadrados*.

   ....

6. Necesito *seis lápices*.

   ....

7. No aprende *porque no presta atención*.

   ....

B.   Complete the following sentences, using the words you have just learned, as needed.

1. El color rojo y el color azul forman (form) el color ....

2. Nosotros coloreamos los rectángulos y .... los cuadrados.

3. No necesito un lápiz azul claro. Necesito un lápiz azul ....

4. El color negro y el color blanco forman el color ....

5. La secretaria trabaja con el director y con el ....

6. La .... trabaja en el hospital.

Lesson 3

En la clase de lenguaje

Los alumnos de la señorita Mena repasan el material para el examen.

MAESTRA —La lección para hoy es un repaso de las partes de la oración.

ANTONIO —¿En qué página están los ejercicios, señorita?

MAESTRA —En la página cuarenta. Deben subrayar los verbos, los nombres y los adjetivos.

TERESA —¿Escribimos oraciones con las palabras nuevas?

MAESTRA —Sí, deben escribir una oración con cada palabra nueva.

TOMÁS —¿Cómo se escribe "Phoenix", maestra?

MAESTRA —Pe–hache–o–e–ene–i–equis.

TOMÁS —¿Con P mayúscula o con minúscula?

MAESTRA —Siempre debes escribir los nombres propios con letra mayúscula.

JORGE —¿Cuándo es el examen de ortografía, maestra?

MAESTRA —El viernes. ¡Ah! Jorge, ¿dónde está tu composición?

JORGE —Está en mi casa. No está terminada.

ALICIA —¿Cuáles son las palabras que debemos aprender para el examen de ortografía?

MAESTRA —Todas. También deben dar el significado de cada una.

TERESA —¿Está bien así, señorita?

MAESTRA —Sí, está muy bien. Tu letra es muy bonita y muy clara.

OSCAR —Mi trabajo está mal, ¿verdad?

MAESTRA —No, la respuesta es correcta, pero debes escribir con más cuidado.

OLGA —Maestra, ¿dónde está el sacapuntas?

MAESTRA —En mi escritorio. Pero, Olga, debes ir a la oficina de la directora.

OLGA —¿Voy ahora o voy después?

MAESTRA —Ahora no. Después de[1] terminar tu trabajo.

RAFAEL —Señorita, ¿cómo se dice "regla" en inglés?

MAESTRA —*Ruler.* Rafael, debes aprender a[2] buscar las palabras en el diccionario. (*a la clase*) Ahora deben guardar los libros. Es la hora del recreo.

✳ ✳ ✳

In the Language Class

TEACHER: Today's lesson is a review of parts of the sentence.

ANTONIO: What page are the exercises on, miss?

TEACHER: On page forty. You must underline the verbs, the nouns and the adjectives.

TERESA: Do we write sentences with the new words?

TEACHER: Yes, you must write a sentence with each new word.

TOMAS: How do you spell "Phoenix", teacher?

---

[1]Spanish uses infinitives after prepositions.

[2]After *aprender,* the preposition *a* is used before the infinitive.

TEACHER:	P–h–o–e–n–i–x.
TOMAS:	With capital P or small P?
TEACHER:	You should always write proper names with capital letters.
JORGE:	When is the spelling test, teacher?
TEACHER:	On Friday. Oh! Jorge, where's your composition?
JORGE:	It's at my home. It's not finished.
ALICIA:	Which are the words that we should learn for the spelling test?
TEACHER:	All of them. You must also give the meaning of each word (one).
TERESA:	Is it okay like this, miss?
TEACHER:	Yes, that (it) is very good. Your handwriting is very pretty and very clear.
OSCAR:	My work is wrong, right?
TEACHER:	No, the answer is correct, but you must write more carefully.
OLGA:	Teacher, where's the pencil sharpener?
TEACHER:	On my desk. But, Olga, you must go to the principal's office.
OLGA:	Shall I go now or later?
TEACHER:	Not now. After you finish your work.
RAFAEL:	Miss, how do you say "regla" in English?
TEACHER:	"Ruler". Rafael, you must learn to look up the words in the dictionary. (*to the class*) Now you must put your books away. It's recess time.

VOCABULARY

COGNATES

el **adjetivo**	adjective	el **material**	material
la **composición**	composition	la **oficina**	office
correcto(-a)	correct	la **parte**	part
el **diccionario**	dictionary	el **verbo**	verb
el **examen**	exam		

NOUNS

el, la **director(-a)** principal, director
la **letra** handwriting, letter
el **nombre, sustantivo** noun
la **oración** sentence
la **ortografía** spelling
el **repaso** review
la **respuesta** answer
el **significado** meaning

VERBS

aprender to learn
buscar to look up, to look for
guardar to put away, to keep
subrayar to underline

ADJECTIVES

bonito(-a) pretty, beautiful
claro(-a) clear
mayúscula capital (letter)

minúscula small (letter)
nuevo(-a) new
terminado(-a) finished

OTHER WORDS AND EXPRESSIONS

ahora now
así like this
bien well, correct, okay
cada each
¿cómo se dice...? how do you say . . .?
¿cómo se escribe...? how do you spell . . .?
con más cuidado more carefully, with more care
cuál(es) which, what
en mi casa at home (lit. at my house)
la **lección para hoy** today's lesson
mal badly, wrong
nombres propios proper nouns
para for

16

LET'S PRACTICE

Give the Spanish equivalent of the words in parentheses.

1. Ella necesita .... hoy.   (*the teacher's dictionary*)

2. El verbo .... una parte de la oración.   (*is*)

3. La directora .... en .... oficina.   (*is/her*)

4. Nosotros .... a San Francisco con .... maestros.
   (*go/our*)

5. Yo no .... número de teléfono.   (*give/my*)

6. Juanito, ¿Dónde .... lápices?   (*are/your*)

7. Yo .... de Nueva York y .... profesores
   .... de Miami.   (*am/my/are*)

8. El .... director. Ahora .... en
   .... oficina.   (*is/our/is/his*)

CONVERSATION

Answer the following questions based on the dialogue:

1. ¿Qué repasan los alumnos de la señorita Mena?

   ....

2. ¿Cuál es la lección para hoy?

   ....

3. ¿En qué página están los ejercicios?

   ....

4. ¿Qué deben subrayar los niños?

   ....

5. ¿Qué día es el examen de ortografía?

   ....

6. ¿Dónde está la composición de Jorge?

   ....

7. ¿Qué palabras deben aprender los niños para el examen?

....

8. ¿Cómo es la letra de Teresa?

....

9. ¿Está mal la respuesta de Oscar?

....

10. ¿Qué debe aprender Rafael?

....

11. ¿Qué debe hacer Oscar?

....

12. ¿Dónde está el sacapuntas?

....

13. ¿Quién debe ir a la oficina de la directora?

....

14. ¿Olga debe ir a la oficina ahora o después?

....

Some additional questions:

15. ¿Escribe Ud. los nombres propios con letra mayúscula o con letra minúscula?

....

16. ¿Son sus respuestas siempre correctas?

....

17. ¿Busca Ud. las palabras nuevas en el diccionario?

....

18. ¿Es clara su letra?

....

19. ¿Escribe Ud. oraciones con cada palabra nueva?

....

20. ¿Guarda Ud. sus papeles en el escritorio?

....

21. ¿Cómo se dice "respuesta" en inglés?

   ....

22. La palabra *bonito*, ¿es un nombre, un adjetivo o un verbo?

   ....

DIALOGUE COMPLETION

Using your imagination and the vocabulary learned in this lesson, complete the missing lines of this dialogue.

El maestro habla con sus alumnos:

MAESTRO —..

JORGE —Sí, señor, mi composición está terminada.

MAESTRO —..

JORGE —Está en su escritorio.

RAÚL —¿Cuándo es el repaso de lenguaje, señor?

MAESTRO —..

RAÚL —¿El jueves? ¿Debemos dar el significado de las palabras nuevas?

MAESTRO —..

RITA —¿Cuántas oraciones debemos escribir con cada palabra?

MAESTRO —..

RITA —Señor, ¿cómo se escribe "bien" en inglés?

MAESTRO —..

TOMÁS —Señor, ¿mi trabajo está bien así?

MAESTRO —..

TOMÁS —¿No? ¿Por qué?

MAESTRO —..

TOMÁS —Señor, yo siempre trabajo con cuidado, pero mi letra no es clara.

SITUATIONAL EXERCISES

What would you say in the following situations?

1. Tell your students they must open the book to page twenty-five. Tell them also that today's lesson is a review of parts of the sentence.

2. Ask your Spanish teacher whether you must underline the verbs or the nouns and adjectives. Ask him also how to say "yellow" in Spanish, and then ask him how to spell it.

3. Ask your Spanish teacher if "*abril*" is spelled with a capital "*a*" or a small "*a*".

4. Tell your students that the spelling test is on Thursday. Tell them they must learn all the new words and give the meaning of each one. Tell them also that they should look up the words in the dictionary.

5. Tell one of your students that the answer is correct but that his handwriting is not clear, and that he must write more carefully.

6. Tell your Spanish teacher that your composition is at your house, and that it is not finished.

7. Tell your students that the pencil sharpener, the ruler, and the dictionary are on your desk. Tell them also that they must put their books and notebooks away after they finish their work.

YOU'RE ON YOUR OWN!

With a classmate, act out the following:

A teacher and a student who is asking questions about assignments, spelling, date of tests, where things are, etc.

VOCABULARY EXPANSION (Optional)

A. *Other parts of speech:*

1. **adverbio** adverb
2. **artículo definido** definite article
3. **artículo indefinido** indefinite article
4. **conjunción** conjunction
5. **interjección** interjection
6. **nombres comunes** common nouns
7. **preposición** preposition

B. *Other terms related to language:*

1. **abreviatura** abbreviation
2. **antónimo** antonym
3. **complemento** object
4. **definición** definition
5. **en orden alfabético** in alphabetical order
6. **futuro** future
7. **pasado** past
8. **predicado** predicate
9. **sinónimo** synonym
10. **sujeto** subject

Do you remember the words used in the Vocabulary Expansion?

A. Say, in Spanish, what parts of speech the following words are.

1. los ....

2. ¡Ah! ....

3. con ....

4. libro ....

5. México ....

6. mal ....

7. y ....

20

8. una ....

9. nuevo ....

B. Complete the following sentences, using the new words.

1. Necesito buscar la .... de las palabras en el diccionario.

2. En la oración "Juan habla español", "Juan" es el .... y "habla

   español" es el ....

3. Debes escribir todas las palabras en ....

4. "I go" está en .... "I went" está en .... "I will

   go" está en ....

5. La .... de "usted" es "Ud."

6. En la oración "Yo llamo a Luis", "Luis" es el ....

7. "Bien" y "mal" no son sinónimos; son ....

Lesson 4

En la clase de geografía

Hoy la maestra viene a clase con mapas y láminas. También tiene un globo terráqueo. La lección de hoy es sobre la geografía de los Estados Unidos.

MAESTRA	—¿En qué continente está situado nuestro país?
CÉSAR	—En América del Norte.
MAESTRA	—¿Cuáles son los límites de los Estados Unidos?
LUPE	—Al norte limita con el Canadá, al sur con México, al este con el océano Atlántico, y al oeste con el océano Pacífico.
MAESTRA	—¡Muy bien! ¡Eres muy inteligente! Y¿cuál es el río más largo de los Estados Unidos?
ROBERTO	—¿El río Missouri?
MAESTRA	—No, el río Mississippi es más largo que el río Missouri. Es el más largo de todos.
SARA	—¡Señorita! La montaña más alta es Mount McKinley, ¿verdad?
MAESTRA	—Sí. ¿Cuántos estados tiene nuestro país y cuál es la población?
JOSÉ	—Tiene cincuenta estados, pero no estoy seguro del número de habitantes.
MAESTRA	—Más o menos doscientos cincuenta millones. ¿Cuál es la capital de los Estados Unidos?
EVA	—¿Nueva York?
MARTA	—¡No! Washington. Allí vive el presidente.
MAESTRA	—Muy bien, Marta. Ahora, tenemos un estado que no está dentro del continente. ¿Cuál es?
RAFAEL	—Hawaii. Mi tío vive allí en la isla de Maui, y viene la semana próxima. Él es profesor.
MAESTRA	—¡Qué bien! ¡Qué contento debes estar! ¿Cuáles son los productos principales que tiene Hawaii?
RAFAEL	—Azúcar y piñas… Y tiene muchos volcanes.
MAESTRA	—Es verdad. Mario, ¿cuál es la superficie de los Estados Unidos?
MARIO	—¿Un millón de millas cuadradas?
MAESTRA	—No, mucho más. Tiene tres millones, seiscientas quince mil, ciento veinte y dos millas las cuadradas.
OLGA	—¡Uy! ¿Es el país más grande del mundo?
MAESTRA	—No, pero es uno de los más grandes. Tiene muchas fuentes de riqueza: la agricultura, la ganadería, la industria, la pesca y las minas.
IRMA	—Señorita, ¿hoy tenemos la práctica de incendios?
MAESTRA	—Sí, y mañana tenemos la práctica de terremoto.

✱   ✱   ✱

In the Geography Class

Today the teacher comes to class with maps and illustrations. She also has a globe. Today's lesson is about the geography of the United States.

TEACHER:	On which continent is our country located?
CESAR:	In North America.

TEACHER:	What are the boundaries of the United States?
LUPE:	To the north, it borders with Canada, to the south, with Mexico, to the east, with the Atlantic Ocean, and to the west with the Pacific Ocean.
TEACHER:	Very good! You're very smart! And which is the longest river in the United States?
ROBERTO:	The Missouri River?
TEACHER:	No, the Mississippi River is longer than the Missouri River. It is the longest one of all.
SARA:	Teacher! The highest mountain is Mount McKinley, right?
TEACHER:	Yes. How many states does our country have, and what is its population?
JOSE:	It has fifty states, but I'm not sure about the number of inhabitants.
TEACHER:	About two hundred and fifty million. What is the capital of the United States?
EVA:	New York?
MARTA:	No! Washington. The president lives there.
TEACHER:	Very good, Marta. Now, we have a state that is not in the continent (continental U.S.). Which is it?
RAFAEL:	Hawaii. My uncle lives there, on the island of Maui, and he is coming next week. He's a professor.
TEACHER:	How nice! How happy you must be! What are the main products that Hawaii has?
RAFAEL:	Sugar and pineapple . . . And it has many volcanoes . . .
TEACHER:	That's true. What's the area of the United States?
MARIO:	One million square miles?
TEACHER:	No, much more. It has three million, six hundred fifteen thousand, one hundred twenty-two square miles.
OLGA:	Wow! Is it the biggest country in the world?
TEACHER:	No, but it is one of the biggest. It has many sources of income: agriculture, livestock, industry, fishing, and mining.
IRMA:	Teacher, do we have fire drill today?
TEACHER:	Yes, and tomorrow earthquake drill.

VOCABULARY

COGNATES

la **agricultura**	agriculture	el **millón**	million
el **Atlántico**	Atlantic	la **mina**	mine
la **capital**	capital	el **monte**	mount
el **continente**	continent	el **océano**	ocean
la **geografía**	geography	el **Pacífico**	Pacific
la **isla**	island	el **producto**	product

NOUNS

el **azúcar** sugar
el **estado** state
los **Estados Unidos** United States
el **este** East
la **ganadería** livestock
el, la **habitante** inhabitant
el **incendio, fuego** fire
la **lámina** picture, illustration
el **límite** boundary
la **milla** mile
la **montaña** mountain
el **mundo** world
el **norte** North
el **número** number
el **oeste** West
el **país** country, nation

la **pesca** fishing
la **piña** pineapple
la **población** population
la **práctica** drill
el **río** river
la **superficie, área** area
el **sur** South
el **terremoto** earthquake
el **tío** uncle

VERBS

limitar to border

ADJECTIVES

alto(-a) high
contento(-a) happy

24

largo(-a)   long
principal   main
seguro(-a)   sure
situado(-a)   situated, located

OTHER WORDS AND EXPRESSIONS
allí   there
América del Norte   North America
dentro   in, inside
fuentes de riqueza   sources of income

globo terráqueo   globe
la semana próxima   next week
limita con...   borders with
mañana   tomorrow
más o menos   about, more or less
que   that
¡qué bien!   how nice!
¡qué contento!   how happy!
sobre   about
¡uy   wow!

LET'S PRACTICE

A.   Complete the following sentences, using one of the following:

de la   a la
de las   a las
del   al
de los   a los

1. Vamos .... Estados Unidos.

2. Es uno .... ríos más largos .... isla.

3. Mi tío va .... montañas.

4. El globo terráqueo es .... profesoras que están allí.

5. México está .... sur .... Estados Unidos.

6. Las láminas son .... maestros.

7. El monte Everest es la montaña más alta .... mundo.

8. Yo voy .... mina.

B.   Establish comparisons using the adjectives in parentheses and adding the corresponding definite articles whenever necessary.

(alto)   el profesor / yo

....

(largo)   río Colorado / río Grande

....

(grande)   mi casa / la escuela

....

(pequeño)   Océano Atlántico / Océano Pacífico

....

25

(difícil)   español / inglés

....

CONVERSATION

Answer the following questions based on the dialogue.

1. ¿Qué tiene la maestra para la clase de hoy?

....

2. ¿Sobre qué es la lección de hoy?

....

3. ¿Está situado nuestro país en la América del Sur?

....

4. ¿Con qué limitan los Estados Unidos al este?

....

5. ¿Cuál es la montaña más alta de los Estados Unidos?

....

6. ¿Está José seguro del número de habitantes de los Estados Unidos?

....

7. ¿Dónde vive el Presidente?

....

8. ¿Es Nueva York la capital de los Estados Unidos?

....

9. ¿Es el río Missouri el río más largo de los Estados Unidos?

....

10. ¿Están dentro del continente todos los estados de los Estados Unidos?

....

11. ¿Por qué debe estar contento Rafael?

....

12. ¿Dónde vive el tío de Rafael?

....

13. ¿Cuáles son la fuentes de riqueza de los Estados Unidos?

....

14. ¿Cuándo tienen los niños la práctica de incendios?

....

Some additional questions:

15. ¿Con qué limita al oeste el estado donde Ud. vive?   (¿Al norte?)

....

16. ¿Cuál es el río más largo del mundo?

....

17. ¿Cuántas millas cuadradas de superficie tiene el estado donde Ud. vive?

....

18. Más o menos, ¿cuántos habitantes tiene su ciudad?

....

19. ¿Tiene Ud. muchas láminas en su clase?

....

20. ¿Cuál es la capital de Venezuela?

....

DIALOGUE COMPLETION

Using your imagination and the vocabulary learned in this lesson complete the missing lines of this dialogue.

En la clase de geografía.

MAESTRA   —Hoy nuestra lección es sobre los Estados Unidos.

RITA   —..

MAESTRA   —No, nuestro país no es el más grande de todos.

MARCOS   —..

MAESTRA   —Tiene más o menos 250 millones de habitantes.   ¿Cuántos estados tiene nuestro país, Raúl?

RAÚL   —..

MAESTRA —¿Qué estado tiene muchos volcanes?

CARMEN —...

MAESTRA —¿Es Hawaii una isla o un continente?

IRENE —...

MAESTRA —¿Cuáles son los principales productos de Hawaii?

LUIS —...

MAESTRA —¿Es la pesca una fuente de riqueza de los Estados Unidos?

CLARA —...

MAESTRA —¡Qué bien! Uds. estudian mucho. Estoy muy contenta.

SITUATIONAL EXERCISES

What would you say in the following situations?

1. Tell your students that today's lesson is about the geography of the United States, and ask them in which continent our country is situated, and what the boundaries of the United States are.
2. Ask your students which is the longest river and the highest mountain in the United States. Ask them also how many states our country has.
3. Tell your students that the United States has about two hundred and fifty million inhabitants, and that it has an area of three million, six hundred fifteen thousand, one hundred twenty-two square miles. Tell them also that the capital is Washington.
4. Tell your students that the United States' main sources of income are: agriculture, livestock, industry, fishing, and mines.
5. Tell your students that you are having fire drill and earthquake drill next week.

YOU'RE ON YOUR OWN!

With a classmate act out the following:

A teacher asking a student questions about the geography of the United States.

VOCABULARY EXPANSION (Optional)

Other words related to geography:

1. **Africa** Africa
2. **América Central** Central America
3. **archipiélago** archipielago
4. **Asia** Asia
5. **cabo** cape
6. **ciclón** cyclone
   cálido warm, hot
7. **clima** **templado** temperate
   climate **frío** cold
8. **cordillera** cordillera, chain of mountains
9. **desierto** desert
10. **Europa** Europe
11. **golfo** gulf
12. **huracán** hurricane
13. **lago** lake
14. **mar** sea
15. **meridiano** meridian
16. **paralelo** parallel
17. **península** peninsula
18. **polos** poles

Do you remember the words used in the Vocabulary Expansion?

Complete the following sentences, using the words you have just learned, as needed:

1. ...., ... y .... son continentes.

2. El Erie es un ....

3. Un .... es un grupo de islas.

4. Las líneas del globo terráqueo son los .... y los ....

5. El Canal de Panamá está en la América ....

6. El Mediterráneo es un ....

7. El .... Kennedy está en la Florida.

8. El Sahara es un ....

9. La Florida es una ....

10. Louisiana limita al sur con el .... de México.

11. No es un huracán. Es un ....

12. Santa Claus vive en el .... Norte.

13. Chile limita al este con la .... de los Andes.

Lesson 5

En la clase de trabajo manual

Hoy los alumnos de segundo grado van a aprender cómo hacer un arbolito de Navidad.

MAESTRA —Niños, hoy vamos a hacer varias cosas con papeles de colores.

BLANCA —Señorita, yo no tengo tijera.[1] ¿Vamos a recortar algo?

MAESTRA —Sí. Hay tijeras y goma de pegar en el armario que está a la derecha.

VÍCTOR —Señorita, tengo sed.

MAESTRA —Debes esperar hasta la hora del recreo para ir al baño y tomar agua.

SILVIA —¿Dónde está el estambre, señorita?

MAESTRA —En el estante de arriba, a la izquierda. Bueno, vamos a empezar.

ELBA —¿Qué color de papel vamos a usar?

MAESTRA —Verde. Primero vamos a doblar el papel por la mitad y dibujar el arbolito.

JAVIER —Yo no tengo el modelo.

MAESTRA —Hay uno en el cajón de mi escritorio.

JAVIER —¿Aquí?

MAESTRA —Sí. (*A la clase*) Deben poner el modelo sobre el papel y trazar una línea alrededor del arbolito.

HILDA —Yo no entiendo, maestra.

MAESTRA —Así, con el papel doblado. (*A la clase*) Ahora deben cortar, siguiendo la línea del dibujo.

RUBÉN —¿Ya está listo?

MAESTRA —No, ahora vamos a recortar círculos pequeños de diferentes colores.

GLORIA —¿Para qué?

MAESTRA —Vamos a pegar los círculos en el arbolito.

YOLANDA —¡Es un arbolito de Navidad! ¡Qué bonito![2]

MAESTRA —Después del recreo vamos a hacer un Santa Claus de fieltro y algodón.

(*Después del recreo, los niños regresan a la clase y continúan la clase de trabajo manual.*)

MAESTRA —¡Jaime! ¡No debes mascar chicle aquí! (*A la clase*) Niños, ya son las tres menos veinte.

JAIME —¿No vamos a terminar el Santa Claus?

MAESTRA —No, ahora van a recoger todas las cosas y limpiar las mesas. Ya es la hora de salida.

✳ ✳ ✳

The Arts and Crafts Class

Today the second-grade students are going to learn how to make a Christmas tree.

TEACHER: Children, today we're going to make several things with colored paper.

BLANCA: Teacher, I don't have (any) scissors. Are we going to cut anything?

---

[1]Notice the omission of the indefinite article after *tener,* used in the negative.

[2]Spanish *que* + adjective: English how + adjective.

31

TEACHER:	Yes. There are scissors and glue in the cabinet (which is) on the right.
VICTOR:	Teacher, I'm thirsty.
TEACHER:	You must wait until recess (time) to go to the bathroom and drink water.
SILVIA:	Where is the yarn, teacher?
TEACHER:	On the top shelf, to the left. Okay, we're going to start.
ELBA:	What color paper are we going to use?
TEACHER:	Green. First, we're going to fold the paper in half and draw the little tree.
JAVIER:	I don't have the pattern.
TEACHER:	There is one in my desk drawer.
JAVIER:	Here?
TEACHER:	Yes. (*To the class*) You must put the pattern on the paper and draw a line around the little tree.
HILDA:	I don't understand, teacher.
TEACHER:	Like this, with the paper folded. (*To the class*) Now you must cut, following the line of the drawing.
RUBÉN:	Is it (already) ready?
TEACHER:	No, we're going to cut out small circles of different colors.
GLORIA:	What for?
TEACHER:	We're going to glue the circles on the little tree.
YOLANDA:	It's a Christmas tree! How pretty!
TEACHER:	After recess we're going to make a felt and cotton Santa Claus.

(*After recess, the children return to the classroom and continue the arts and crafts class.*)

TEACHER:	Jaime! You shouldn't chew gum here! (*To the class*) Children, it's (already) twenty to three.
JAIME:	Aren't we going to finish the Santa Claus?
TEACHER:	No. Now you're going to pick up everything and clean the tables. It's time to go.

VOCABULARY

COGNATES

diferente different   la **línea** line

NOUNS

el[1] **agua** (*f.*) water
el **algodón** cotton
el **arbolito** little tree
el **armario** cabinet
el **cajón,** la **gaveta** drawer
la **cosa** thing
el **chicle,** la **goma de mascar** chewing gum
el **dibujo** drawing
el **estambre,** la **lana de tejer** yarn
el **estante** shelf
el **fieltro** felt
la **goma de pegar** glue
la **mitad** half
el **modelo, patrón** pattern
la **Navidad** Christmas
la **tijera** scissors

VERBS

continuar to continue
cortar to cut
dibujar to draw

doblar to fold
hacer[2] to do, to make
limpiar to clean
mascar to chew
pegar to glue
poner[2] to put
recoger (yo recojo) to pick up
recortar to cut, to trim
regresar to return, to go (come) back
tomar to drink
trazar to draw (i.e., a line)
usar to use

ADJECTIVES

doblado(-a) folded
listo(-a) ready
pequeño(-a) small, little
varios(-as) several, various

OTHER WORDS AND EXPRESSIONS

a la derecha to the right
a la izquierda to the left

[1]El (un) when the word that follows starts with stressed **a** or **ha.**
[2]These verbs will be conjugated in lesson 7.

algo   something
alrededor (de)   around
de arriba   top, upper
hasta   until
hora de salida   time to go, quitting time

por la mitad   in half
¡qué bonito(-a)!   how pretty
¿qué color de...?   what color
siguiendo   following
trabajo manual   arts and crafts

LET'S PRACTICE

A.   Make sentences using the elements given.   Follow the model.

Modelo: yo / querer / recortar / arbolito
　　　　Yo quiero recortar el arbolito.

1. nosotros / no querer / limpiar / mesas

   ....

2. ellos / preferir / regresar / cuatro y media

   ....

3. Roberto / cerrar / ventanas / puertas

   ....

4. niños / empezar a / cortar / patrón

   ....

5. clase / comenzar / ocho / la mañana

   ....

6. Yolanda / perder / tijeras

   ....

7. ¿? / tú / entender / lección

   ....

8. nosotros / cerrar / puertas

   ....

B.   Complete the following sentences, using *ir a* and appropriate verbs, as needed.

1. Los niños .... la clase

   después del recreo.

2. Yo .... el papel por la

   mitad.

3. Nosotros .... agua.

4. ¿Tú .... un Santa Claus de fieltro?

5. Elsa .... el estambre en el armario.

6. ¿Ud. .... chicle?

7. Uds. .... una línea.

8. Mario .... los círculos de papel en el arbolito.

CONVERSATION

Answer the following questions based on the dialogue.

1. ¿Qué van a aprender hoy los alumnos de segundo grado?

....

2. Blanca va a necesitar una tijera. ¿Por qué?

....

3. ¿Dónde hay tijeras y goma de pegar?

....

4. ¿El armario está a la derecha o a la izquierda?

....

5. ¿Hasta cuándo debe esperar Víctor para ir al baño y tomar agua?

....

6. ¿Dónde está la lana de tejer?

....

7. ¿Van a usar papel rojo los niños?

....

8. ¿Qué van a hacer los niños primero?

....

9. ¿Dónde hay un modelo del arbolito?

....

10. Después de poner el modelo sobre el papel, ¿qué deben hacer?

....

11. ¿Cómo deben cortar el papel?

....

12. ¿Qué van a hacer los niños con los círculos de diferentes colores?

....

13. ¿Qué van a hacer los niños después del recreo?

....

Some additional questions:

14. ¿Tiene usted clases de trabajo manual?

....

15. ¿Qué hora es?

....

16. ¿Va a terminar usted la clase de español?

....

17. ¿Después de una clase de trabajo manual, recoge usted todas las cosas?

....

18. ¿Va a limpiar usted las mesas?

....

19. ¿A qué hora es la hora de salida?

....

20. ¿Mascan sus alumnos chicle en clase?

....

DIALOGUE COMPLETION

Use your imagination and the vocabulary learned in this lesson to complete the missing parts of these dialogues:

La maestra y Javier:

MAESTRA — ....

JAVIER	—No, no tengo goma de pegar. ¿Dónde están todas las cosas?
MAESTRA	—..
JAVIER	—¿En el cajón de arriba?
MAESTRA	—..
JAVIER	—¿Papel verde? ¿Por qué? ¿Qué vamos a hacer?
MAESTRA	—..
JAVIER	—¿Vamos a hacer un Santa Claus de fieltro también?
MAESTRA	—..
JAVIER	—Sí, sí... hay algodón y fieltro en el estante de arriba.
MAESTRA	—..

La maestra y Nora:

NORA	—..
MAESTRA	—Debes esperar hasta la hora del recreo para tomar agua.
NORA	—..
MAESTRA	—Después del recreo vamos a continuar el arbolito.
NORA	—..
MAESTRA	—Son las dos menos cuarto.

SITUATIONAL EXERCISES

What would you say in the following situations?

1. Tell your students that you are going to make a little Christmas tree.   Tell them also that there is cotton in the drawer.
2. You are giving instructions on how to make the little tree.   Tell your students they must:
   a) fold the paper in half, b) put the pattern on the paper and draw the tree, c) cut, following the line of the drawing.
3. One of your students is chewing gum in class.   Tell him he shouldn't chew gum in class. Someone tells you he/she is thirsty.   Tell him/her that's what recess is for: to get a drink of water and go to the bathroom.
4. Your students are done with their work and the classroom is messy.   Tell them they should pick everything up and clean the table and their desks.   Tell them it is time to go.

YOU'RE ON YOUR OWN!

With a classmate, act out the following:

A teacher is instructing a student on how to make things.   All the necessary material should be brought to class.   With the help of your instructor, see if you can make something else besides a little Christmas tree.

VOCABULARY EXPANSION (Optional)

A.   Other words and phrases that may be used in art classes:

la **acuarela**   watercolor
la **aguja**   needle
el **cartón**   cardboard
la **cartulina**   construction paper
el **compás**   compass
el **hilo**   thread
la **línea de puntos**   dotted line

el **pincel**   brush
la **pintura**   paint
calcar   to trace
coser   to sew
desdoblar   to unfold
pintar   to paint
unir los puntos   connect the dots

B.   Useful vocabulary to describe location, position, etc.

arriba   up, upstairs
abajo   down, downstairs
encima de   on top of
debajo de   under

adentro   inside
afuera   outside
delante (de)   in front of
detrás (de)   behind

Do you remember the words included in the Vocabulary Expansion?

A.   Answer in the negative, giving opposites.

1. ¿Estás *detrás de* la casa?

   ....

2. ¿Está *arriba*?

   ....

3. ¿Está *debajo del* escritorio?

   ....

4. ¿Está *afuera*?

   ....

B.   Complete the following sentences appropriately.

1. Para coser necesito .... y ....

2. No vamos a usar .... ; vamos a usar cartulina.

3. Para pintar necesitamos la .... y los ....

4. Para hacer un círculo necesito un ....

5. Debes firmar en la línea de ....

6. La .... es una pintura de agua.

7. No vamos a calcar el arbolito. Vamos a unir los ....

8. Vamos a .... el papel y cortar por la línea de puntos.

VOCABULARY REVIEW

A. Circle the word or phrase that does not belong in each group.

1. la agricultura, la pesca, el terremoto
2. el cuadrado, el círculo, el rectángulo
3. el tío, la página, el papel
4. triángulo, palabras, vocabulario
5. estante, agua, armario
6. dibujar, trazar, regresar
7. recortar, sumar, multiplicar
8. sobresaliente, doblado, satisfactorio
9. rosado, anaranjado, listo
10. ¿cómo se escribe...?, baño, ortografía
11. milla, monte, montaña
12. población, habitantes, mina
13. mapa, piña, globo terráqueo
14. aquí, allí, bueno
15. mitad, algodón, fieltro

B. Circle the word or phrase that best completes each sentence.

1. El azúcar es (una lámina, un producto, un número) de Hawaii.
2. ¡Qué contento estoy! Hoy no (escucho, llevo, voy) a la escuela.
3. Ahora necesito (el arbolito, la conversación, la lista) de los niños que están presentes.
4. No trabajamos mucho. Tenemos (muy bien, muy poco, muy bonito) trabajo.
5. Su hijo estudia, pero nunca (participa, dobla, pone) en clase.
6. El fieltro está en el cajón de (alrededor, arriba, agua).
7. Es la hora de lectura. Los niños (borran, llaman, leen).
8. Primero buscamos el significado de las palabras en (el material, el diccionario, la cosa).
9. Después deben copiar los números en el cuaderno de (láminas, ayudas, ejercicios).
10. Es la hora del recreo. ¿Quién necesita (nombres propios, ir al baño, más o menos)?
11. Hoy es el veinticinco de diciembre. Es (la semana próxima, la tabla de multiplicar, Navidad).
12. ¿Quiénes deben (firmar, limpiar, aprender) la libreta de calificaciones?
13. Si ya tienen la respuesta correcta, deben (pasar lista, levantar la mano, leer más).
14. No leemos porque no tenemos (secretario, oficina, libro de lectura).
15. Todos ustedes estudian mucho. ¡Qué (bonito, bien, largo)!
16. Debes escribir con más (cuidado, límite, dibujo).
17. Es la hora de salida. Debemos terminar (el repaso, el sustantivo, la atención).
18. ¿Qué color de (papel, lectura, tarea) necesitamos para la clase de trabajo manual?

19. Es una ciudad muy importante.   Es la ciudad (segura, principal, diferente).

20. Debes (recoger, tomar, doblar) el papel por la mitad.

21. ¡Un momento!   Todavía no está (nuevo, varios, terminado).

22. Ella siempre me llama por (instrucción, verdad, teléfono).

23. ¿Tiene (algún, sobre, cada) problema con Pepito?

24. Tu letra no es muy (así, clara, contenta).

C.   Match the questions in column A with the answers in column B.

A

1. ¿Trabaja mejor con los demás?
2. ¿Qué debo hacer para mejorar?
3. ¿Dónde estudiamos hoy?
4. ¿Cómo se dice *until*?
5. ¿Vas a tu casa?
6. ¿Para qué necesitas el lápiz rojo?
7. ¿Cómo están?
8. ¿Tienen práctica de terremoto?
9. ¿Dónde está el director?
10. ¿Qué debemos repasar?
11. ¿Cómo dibujamos el arbolito?
12. ¿Dónde guardan la lana?
13. ¿Yo debo continuar con el grupo?
14. ¿Necesitas algo?
15. ¿Cuál es tu libro?
16. ¿Qué debo traer?

B

a. Para subrayar los verbos.
b. La lección para hoy.
c. Dentro de la gaveta.
d. Sí, un lápiz azul.
e. El libro que está sobre la mesa.
f. Prestar más atención.
g. Las láminas.
h. En clase.
i. Sí, y Carlos también.
j. Hasta.
k. Bien.
l. No, independientemente.
m. Siguiendo la línea de puntos.
n. Sí, porque debo escribir una composición.
o. Sí, a veces.
p. En mi casa.

D.   Crucigrama

HORIZONTAL

1. opuesto (*opposite*) de *incorrecto*
3. Para pegar uso _____ de pegar
9. No se escribe con letra mayúscula; se escribe con letra _____ .
10. La ganadería es una _____ de riqueza.
11. La maestra trabaja en la _____ .
12. "Pequeño" no es un verbo; es un _____ .
14. cajón
16. superficie
18. nombre
20. Para cortar necesito la _____ .
21. El adjetivo es una parte de la _____ .
22. dar color
23. mil × mil = un _____

25. goma de mascar
27. opuesto de *sumar*
28. Hawaii es una _____ .
29. Wáshington es la _____ de los Estados Unidos.
30. El azul y el _____ forman el color verde.
35. No está a la derecha; está a la _____ .
36. fuego
37. opuesto de *norte*
39. Los niños estudian mucho porque tienen un _____ .
40. Mt. Everest es la _____ más alta del mundo.

VERTICAL

1. Asia es un ____ .

2. En la clase de ____ , estudiamos los ríos de Europa.

4. opuesto de *este*

5. Estados Unidos está situado en la ____ del Norte.

6. patrón

7. ¿Qué significa la palabra "uy"? Necesito un ____ .

8. Los estudiantes comen en la ____ .

13. ¿Qué ____ es hoy? ¿El 3 de septiembre?

15. No deben leer en voz alta. Deben leer en ____ .

17. California es un ____ .

19. El Pacífico y el ____ son océanos.

23. Los niños ____ chicle.

24. color café

26. lana de tejer

31. Estados Unidos ____ al norte con Canadá.

32. opuesto de *mal*

33. México es un ____ .

34. Hoy es martes; ____ es miércoles.

38. El Nilo es un ____ de Egipto.

Lesson 6

Un repaso de anatomía

La semana próxima los niños van a tener varios exámenes. El lunes tienen uno de anatomía. Hoy repasan las lecciones.

MAESTRA	—Hoy vamos a repasar anatomía. ¿Alguien recuerda cómo se llama la armazón que sostiene el cuerpo? ¿Mario?
MARIO	—Se llama esqueleto y está formado por los huesos.
MAESTRA	—¡Muy bien! ¿Qué es una coyuntura?
ESTELA	—Es la unión de dos o más huesos.
MAESTRA	—Muy bien, pero hay que levantar la mano antes de contestar.
JOSÉ	—¿La rodilla es una articulación?
MAESTRA	—Sí, y también el codo. Bueno, ¿qué mueve los huesos? ¿Rosa?
ROSA	—¿La sangre?
MAESTRA	—No es la sangre, Rosa. Tienes que estudiar más... ¿Anita?
ANITA	—Los músculos. La sangre no mueve nada.
MAESTRA	—¿Qué cubre todo nuestro cuerpo? ¿Gonzalo?
GONZALO	—La ropa.
RAQUEL	—No, no... Tú nunca contestas bien. Es la piel.
MAESTRA	—Muy bien. La piel protege el cuerpo de los microbios.
JUAN	—Señorita, ¿por qué hay distintos colores de piel?
MAESTRA	—Porque el color de la piel depende de la cantidad de pigmento. Si una persona tiene mucho pigmento, la piel es oscura, si tiene poco, es muy clara.
PACO	—¿Con qué pensamos, señorita?
MAESTRA	—Con el cerebro. El cerebro está dentro de la cabeza, protegido por los huesos del cráneo.
RITA	—Cuando comemos, ¿a dónde va la comida?
MAESTRA	—Primero masticamos y tragamos; después la comida va al estómago y de allí a los intestinos, donde termina la digestión.
RITA	—Cuando yo como mucho, siempre duermo.
MAESTRA	—Sí, porque tu cuerpo tiene que trabajar mucho para digerir toda la comida.

(*Suena el timbre para la salida.*)

MAESTRA	—Mañana continuamos con la segunda parte. Gonzalo, ¿vas a repasar la lección conmigo?
GONZALO	—Sí, señorita.

✳   ✳   ✳

A Review of Anatomy

Next week the children are going to have several tests. On Monday they are having one in anatomy. Today they review the lessons.

TEACHER: Today we are going to review anatomy. Does anybody remember what the frame that holds the body is called? Mario?

MARIO:	It's called the skeleton and it's made up of bones.
TEACHER:	Very good! What are the joints?
ESTELA:	It is the joining of two or more bones.
TEACHER:	Very good, but before answering you must raise your hand.
JOSÉ:	Is the knee a joint?
TEACHER:	Yes, and also the elbow. Okay, what moves the bones? Rosa?
ROSA:	The blood . . .?
TEACHER:	It's not the blood, Rosa. You should study more . . . Anita?
ANITA:	The muscles. The blood doesn't move anything.
TEACHER:	What covers all our body? Gonzalo?
GONZALO:	Clothes.
RAQUEL:	No, no. You never answer right. It's the skin.
TEACHER:	Very good. The skin protects the body against germs.
JUAN:	Miss, why are there different colors of skin?
TEACHER:	Because the color of the skin depends on the amount of pigment. If a person has a lot of pigment the skin is dark, if she/he has little (pigment) it is very light.
PACO:	What do we think with, Miss?
TEACHER:	We think with the brain. The brain is inside the head, protected by the bones of the skull.
RITA:	When we eat, where does the food go?
TEACHER:	First we chew and swallow, then the food goes to the stomach and from there to the intestines, where digestion ends.
RITA:	When I eat a lot (much) I always sleep.
TEACHER:	Yes, because your body has to work a great deal in order to digest all the food.

(*The bell rings for dismissal.*)

TEACHER:	Tomorrow we will continue with the second part. Gonzalo, are you going to review the lesson with me?
GONZALO:	Yes, Miss.

VOCABULARY

COGNATES

la **anatomía**	anatomy	la **persona**	person
la **digestión**	digestion	el **pigmento**	pigment
el **intestino**	intestine		

NOUNS

la **armazón**	frame
la **cabeza**	head
la **cantidad**	quantity
el **cerebro**	brain
el **codo**	elbow
la **comida**	food
la **coyuntura, articulación**	joint
el **cráneo**	skull
el **cuerpo**	body
el **esqueleto**	skeleton
el **estómago**	stomach
el **hueso**	bone
el **microbio**	germ
el **músculo**	muscle
la **piel**	skin
la **rodilla**	knee
la **ropa**	clothes
la **sangre**	blood

el **timbre**	bell
la **unión**	joining together

VERBS

cubrir	to cover
depender	to depend
digerir (e:ie)	to digest
masticar	to chew
mover (o:ue)	to move
pensar (e:ie)	to think
proteger (yo protejo)	to protect
sonar (o:ue)	to ring
sostener (*conj. like* **tener**)	to support, to hold
tragar	to swallow

ADJECTIVES

distinto(-a)	different
oscuro(-a)	dark

protegido(-a)   protected

OTHER WORDS AND EXPRESSIONS

antes de   before

¿cómo se llama…?   what is . . . called?
está formado(-a)   is made up, is formed
levantar la mano   to raise one's hand
para la salida   for dismissal

LET'S PRACTICE

Complete the following sentences with the Spanish version of the words in parentheses:

1. Los niños .... van a .... domingos.

   (*never / school / on*)

2. La piel protege el cuerpo de ....   (*germs*)

3. A las tres .... el timbre.   (*rings*)

4. .... masticar bien .... tragar.   (*One must / before*)

5. Los niños .... las partes del ....

   (*have to study / body*)

6. La ropa no es .... , es .... , Pepito.   (*for me / for you*)

7. Los músculos .... los ....   (*move / bones*)

8. Nosotros no .... mover la ....   (*can / head*)

9. Yo .... mastico .... bien.   (*never / nothing*)

10. El cerebro .... bien ....   (*has to be / protected*)

CONVERSATION

Answer the following questions based on the dialogue.

1. ¿Qué van a tener los niños la semana próxima?

   ....

2. ¿Qué día es el examen de anatomía?

   ....

3. ¿Qué repasan los niños hoy?

   ....

4. ¿Cómo se llama la armazón que sostiene el cuerpo?

   ....

5. ¿De qué está formado el esqueleto?

   ....

6. ¿Cómo se llama la unión de dos o más huesos?

   ....

7. ¿Qué hay que hacer antes de contestar?

   ....

8. ¿Quién tiene que estudiar más?

   ....

9. ¿Qué protege la piel?

   ....

10. ¿De qué depende el color de la piel de una persona?

   ....

11. Si una persona tiene mucha cantidad de pigmento, ¿cómo es su piel?

   ....

12. ¿Dónde está el cerebro?

   ....

13. ¿Qué protegen los huesos del cráneo?

   ....

14. ¿Qué son el codo y la rodilla?

   ....

15. Cuando comemos, ¿qué hacemos primero, masticamos o tragamos?

   ....

16. ¿Dónde termina la digestión?

   ....

Some personal questions:

17. ¿Digiere Ud. bien la comida?

....

18. ¿Mastica Ud. bien la comida antes de tragar?

....

19. ¿Piensa Ud. en español o en inglés?

    ....

20. ¿Es su piel oscura o clara?

    ....

21. ¿De qué color es la sangre?

    ....

22. ¿Cuántos huesos hay en el cráneo?

    ....

23. Cuando Ud. come mucho, ¿siempre duerme?

    ....

24. ¿A qué hora suena el timbre para la salida?

    ....

DIALOGUE COMPLETION

Using your imagination and the vocabulary learned in this lesson, complete the missing lines of this dialogue.

En la clase de anatomía:

JULIA   —..

MAESTRA   —El examen de anatomía es el jueves.

JULIA   —..

MAESTRA   —Sí, hoy vamos a repasar.   ¿Tienen algunas preguntas?

TERESA   —..

MAESTRA   —Depende de la cantidad de pigmento de la piel.

DARÍO   —..

MAESTRA   —No, no termina en el estómago; termina en el intestino.

CARMEN   —..

MAESTRA   —Los huesos del cráneo.

ESTER   —..

MAESTRA   —Se llama esqueleto.

ÁNGEL   — ....

MAESTRA   —Sí, el codo es una articulación.   Bueno, mañana continuamos con el repaso.

SITUATIONAL EXERCISES

What would you say in the following situations?

1. Tell your students that they have to review anatomy next week.
2. Ask your students the following questions:
   a. What is a joint?
   b. What covers the body?
   c. Where does food go when we eat?
   d. Why are there different colors of skin?
3. Tell the children one must raise one's hand before answering.
4. Ask a student if she wants to review the lesson with you.   Tell her you can study with her.

YOU'RE ON YOUR OWN!

With a classmate act out the following situation:

A teacher asking a student questions about anatomy.

VOCABULARY EXPANSION (Optional)

Other words related to anatomy:

la **cara**   face
el **cuello**   neck
el **dedo**   finger
el **dedo del pie**   toe
los **dientes**   teeth
la **espalda**   back
la **lengua**   tongue
la **mano**   hand

la **nariz**   nose
el **oído**   inner ear
el **ojo**   eye
la **oreja**   ear
el **pecho**   chest
el **pelo, cabello**   hair
el **pie**   foot
el **tobillo**   ankle

Do you remember the words used in the Vocabulary Expansion?

Name the following parts of the body.

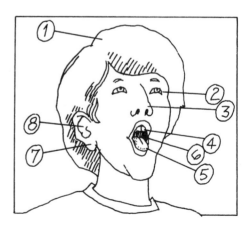

1.	11. ....
2.	12. ....
3.	13. ....
4.	14. ....
5.	15. ....
6.	16. ....
7.	17. ....
8.	18. ....
9.	19. ....
10.	20. ....

Lesson 7

Un repaso de anatomía (II)

Hoy la maestra sigue con el repaso de anatomía, porque los niños dicen que todavía no están listos para el examen.

MAESTRA	—Cecilia, ¿puedes nombrar las partes del aparato respiratorio?
CECILIA	—No sé cuáles son, señorita.
MANUEL	—Yo lo sé… son la nariz, la tráquea, los bronquios y los pulmones.
MAESTRA	—Muy bien. Ahora, como Uds. saben, se necesita oxígeno para vivir. ¿Qué pasa cuando respiramos? ¿Alicia?
ALICIA	—Los pulmones toman el oxígeno para purificar la sangre.
MAESTRA	—¿De qué aparato forma parte la sangre? Roberto, ¿tú lo sabes?
ROBERTO	—Sí, la sangre forma parte del aparato circulatorio.
MAESTRA	—Muy bien. También el corazón, las arterias, las venas y los vasos capilares, como pueden ver en esta lámina…
OLGA	—Yo no la veo bien, señorita…
MAESTRA	—Puedes venir aquí al frente. Carlos, ¿por qué es importante el corazón?
CARLOS	—Porque es el órgano que envía la sangre a todo el cuerpo.
NICOLÁS	—Yo conozco a un hombre que sufre del corazón y ahora van a operarlo.
GERARDO	—¿Se puede vivir sin el corazón?
MAESTRA	—No, lo necesitamos para poder vivir… Margarita, ¿qué elementos forman la sangre?
MARGARITA	—Los glóbulos rojos, los glóbulos blancos y las plaquetas.
MAESTRA	—Muy bien. ¿Para qué sirven las plaquetas?
DAVID	—Para coagular la sangre.
MAESTRA	—Muy bien. Bueno, mañana traigo una lámina para estudiar el sistema nervioso. Ahora vamos a almorzar. Es la hora del almuerzo.

✳   ✳   ✳

A Review of Anatomy

Today the teacher continues with the review of anatomy, because the children say that they are not ready for the exam yet.

TEACHER:	Cecilia, can you name the parts of the respiratory system?
CECILIA:	I don't know which ones they are, Miss.
MANUEL:	I know . . . they are the nose, the trachea, the bronchial tubes and the lungs.
TEACHER:	Very good. Now, as you know, one needs oxygen to live. What happens when we breathe? Alicia?
ALICIA:	The lungs take the oxygen to purify the blood.
TEACHER:	Of what system is the blood a part? Roberto, do you know?
ROBERTO:	Yes, the blood is part of the circulatory system.
TEACHER:	Very good. Also the heart, the arteries, the veins, and the capillary vessels, as you can see in this illustration . . .

OLGA:	I can't see it, teacher.
TEACHER:	You can come here to the front. Carlos, why is the heart important?
CARLOS:	Because it is the organ which sends blood to the whole body.
NICOLÁS:	I know a man who has heart trouble and now they're going to operate on him.
GERARDO:	Can one live without the heart?
TEACHER:	No, we need it to be able to live . . . Margarita, what elements form the blood?
MARGARITA:	The red corpuscles, the white corpuscles and the blood platelets.
TEACHER:	Very good. What are blood platelets good for?
DAVID:	To coagulate the blood.
TEACHER:	Very good. Okay, tomorrow I'll bring an illustration to study the nervous system. Now let's go eat. It's lunch time.

VOCABULARY

COGNATES

la **arteria**	artery	el **oxígeno**	oxygen
el **elemento**	element	la **vena**	vein
el **órgano**	organ		

NOUNS

el **aparato circulatorio**   circulatory system
el **aparato respiratorio**   respiratory system
los **bronquios**   bronchial tubes
el **corazón**   heart
los **glóbulos**   corpuscles
los **glóbulos blancos**   white corpuscles
los **glóbulos rojos**   red corpuscles
la **plaqueta**   blood platelet
los **pulmones**   lungs
el **sistema nervioso**   nervous system
la **tráquea**   windpipe, trachea
los **vasos capilares**   capillary vessels

VERBS

almorzar (o:ue)   to have lunch
coagular   to coagulate
enviar   to send
formar   to form
nombrar   to name

operar   to operate
pasar   to happen
purificar   to purify
respirar   to breathe
tomar   to take

ADJECTIVES

listo(a)   ready
todo(a)   all

OTHER WORDS AND EXPRESSIONS

al frente (de)   to the front (of)
como...   as . . .
formar parte (de)   to be (a) part (of)
la **hora del almuerzo**   lunch time
sin   without
sufrir del corazón   to have heart trouble
vamos a comer   let's eat, let's go eat

LET'S PRACTICE!

Rewrite the following sentences, using the new elements.

1. Yo *visito* a esa señora.   (*conocer*)

   ....

2. *Nosotros* servimos la comida.   (*Ellos*)

   ....

52

3. Yo no *necesito* nada.   (*saber*)

   ....

4. *Uds.* siguen estudiando el sistema nervioso.   (*Nosotros*)

   ....

5. Yo no *escribo* nunca.   (*salir*)

   ....

6. *Ella* dice que sufre del corazón.   (*Yo*)

   ....

7. *Ella* viene al frente porque no ve nada.   (*Yo*)

   ....

8. ¿Para qué sirven las *plaquetas*?   (*la tráquea*)

   ....

9. *Ellos* piden una lámina de las arterias y las venas.   (*Nosotros*)

   ....

10. *Traduzco* las lecciones.   (*Traer*)

   ....

CONVERSATION

Answer the following questions based on the dialogue.

1. ¿Sabe Cecilia cuáles son las partes del aparato respiratorio?

   ....

2. ¿Qué pasa cuando respiramos?

   ....

3. ¿De qué aparato forman parte los vasos capilares?

   ....

4. ¿Cuál es el órgano que envía la sangre a todo el cuerpo?

   ....

5. ¿A quién van a operar del corazón?

   ....

6. ¿Qué elementos forman la sangre?

   ....

7. ¿Para qué sirven las plaquetas?

   ....

8. Es la hora del almuerzo. ¿Qué van a hacer los niños?

   ....

Some additional questions:

9. ¿Repasa Ud. con sus alumnos antes de un examen?

   ....

10. ¿Ve Ud. bien?

   ....

11. ¿Tiene Ud. láminas del sistema nervioso?

   ....

12. ¿A qué hora almuerza Ud.?

   ....

13. Tengo hambre. ¿Ya vamos a comer?

   ....

14. ¿Podemos vivir sin oxígeno? ¿Por qué?

   ....

15. ¿Está Ud. listo(a) para el examen?

   ....

DIALOGUE COMPLETION

Using your imagination and the vocabulary you learned in this lesson, complete the missing lines of this dialogue.

La señorita Vázquez continúa con el repaso de anatomia:

MAESTRA —Elsa, ¿puedes nombrar las partes del aparato circulatorio?

ELSA —..

MAESTRA —Muy bien. ¿Quién sabe cuales son los elementos que forman la sangre?

RAÚL —..

MAESTRA —¿Cuál es el órgano que envía la sangre a todo el cuerpo?

54

RAMIRO —..

MAESTRA —¿Cuáles son las partes del aparato respiratorio.

AURORA —..

MAESTRA —No, el corazón no es parte del aparto respiratorio.

CARMELA —..

MAESTRA —Los pulmones toman el oxígeno para purificar el aire.

RAFAEL —..

MAESTRA —No, no podemos vivir sin el corazón. Bueno, creo que están listos para el examen.

SITUATIONAL EXERCISES

What would you say in the following situations?

1. You are summarizing a lesson on anatomy. You remind your students that:
   a. The nose, the trachea, the bronchial tubes and the lungs are part of the respiratory system.
   b. When we breathe, the lungs take oxygen to purify the blood.
   c. The blood, the heart, the arteries, the veins and the capillary vessels are part of the circulatory system.
   d. The elements that form the blood are: the red corpuscles, the white corpuscles and the blood platelets, which serve to coagulate the blood.
2. Tell the children they need to review the lesson if they want to be ready for the exam.

YOU'RE ON YOUR OWN!

With a classmate, act out the following:

Two students quizzing each other before an anatomy exam

VOCABULARY EXPANSION (Optional)

Other words related to anatomy:

el **aparato digestivo** (digestive system)
- la **boca**   mouth
- el **esófago**   esophagus
- el **estómago**   stomach
- el **intestino delgado**   small intestine
- el **intestino grueso**   large intestine

las **glándulas anexas** (annexed glands)
- las **glándulas salivales**   salivary glands
- el **páncreas**   pancreas
- el **hígado**   liver

el **sistema nervioso** (nervous system)
- el **cerebro**   brain
- el **cerebelo**   cerebellum
- la **médula espinal**   spinal cord
- el **nervio**   nerve

los **sentidos** (senses)	la **vista**	sight
	el **oído**	sense of hearing
	el **olfato**	sense of smell
	el **tacto**	sense of touch
	el **gusto**	sense of taste

Do you remember the words used in the Vocabulary Expansion?

Complete the following sentences, using the words you have just learned, as needed.

1. La comida va de la boca al .... y después al ....

2. Los cinco sentidos son la .... , el .... , el

   .... , el .... y el ....

3. El estómago y el intestino son partes del ....

4. El intestino .... es más largo que el intestino ....

5. El cerebro, el .... , la médula .... y los nervios, forman

   parte del sistema ....

6. Las glándulas .... , el páncreas y el .... son glándulas

   .... al aparato digestivo.

Lesson 8

Una clase de zoología

Hoy la maestra está explicándoles a los niños las diferentes clases de animales que existen en el mundo.

MAESTRA —El reino animal se divide en dos grandes grupos: el tipo de los vertebrados y el tipo de los invertebrados.

ÁNGEL —¿Los peces son invertebrados, señorita?

MAESTRA —No. Los invertebrados no tienen columna vertebral. Los insectos son invertebrados.

INÉS —Los mamíferos son vertebrados, ¿verdad, señorita?

MAESTRA —¡Muy bien, Inés! Las aves, los reptiles, los anfibios y los peces también pertenecen a ese grupo.

MARÍA —¿Qué es un anfibio?

MAESTRA —Un animal que en la primera parte de su vida vive en el agua y respira como los peces, y después como los mamíferos.

DIEGO —¡Como los renacuajos, que después son ranas! Yo tengo dos... Le voy a preguntar a mi mamá si puedo traerlas.

MAESTRA —Puedes traerlas mañana, si quieres. ¿Y los reptiles? ¿Cuáles son?

ANITA —Las serpientes, las lagartijas, los cocodrilos y las tortugas.

CARMEN —Las aves también son reptiles.

LUIS —¡Eso no es verdad! Las aves pueden volar.

MAESTRA —Muy bien, Luis. ¿Cuáles son las características de las aves?

OLGA —¡Yo puedo decírselas! Tienen plumas y la boca en forma de pico.

MAESTRA —¡Eso es! En esta lámina vemos fotografías de diferentes clases de aves.

ANTONIO —¡Yo sé otra cosa! Las aves nacen de huevos.

MAESTRA —Sí, y los mamíferos nacen vivos. ¿Qué otras características tienen los mamíferos?

OSCAR —Tienen sangre caliente y el cuerpo cubierto de pelos.

MAESTRA —¿Y los peces?

TERESA —Tienen sangre fría, el cuerpo cubierto de escamas y respiran por branquias.

MAESTRA —¡Muy bien! En nuestra biblioteca hay varios libros sobre animales. Se los pueden pedir a la señorita Roca.

$$* \quad * \quad *$$

A Zoology Class

Today the teacher is explaining to the children the different kinds of animals that exist in the world.

TEACHER: The animal kingdom is divided into two large groups: the type of the vertebrates and the type of the invertebrates.

ANGEL: Are fish invertebrates, teacher?

TEACHER: No. Invertebrates don't have a spine. Insects are invertebrates.

INES: Mammals are vertebrates, right teacher?

TEACHER:	Very good, Ines! Birds, reptiles, amphibians, and fish also belong to that group.
MARIA:	What is an amphibian?
TEACHER:	An animal that, in the first part of his life, lives in the water and breathes like fish (do), and then like mammals (do).
DIEGO:	Like tadpoles, which are frogs afterwards! I have two . . . I'm going to ask my mother if I can bring them.
TEACHER:	You can bring them tomorrow, if you want to. And reptiles? Which ones are they?
ANITA:	Snakes, lizards, crocodiles and turtles.
CARMEN:	Birds are reptiles too.
LUIS:	That's not true! Birds can fly.
TEACHER:	Very good, Luis. What are the characteristics of birds?
OLGA:	I can tell (them to) you! They have feathers and the mouth is shaped like a beak.
TEACHER:	That's it! In this illustration we see pictures of different kinds of birds.
ANTONIO:	I know something else! Birds are born from eggs.
TEACHER:	Yes, and mammals are born alive. What other characteristics do mammals have?
OSCAR:	They have warm blood and their bodies (are) covered with hair.
TEACHER:	And fish?
TERESA:	They are cold blooded, their bodies (are) covered with scale and they breathe through branchiae.
TEACHER:	Very good! In our library there are several books about animals. You can ask Miss Roca for them.

VOCABULARY

COGNATES

el **anfibio**	amphibian	el **insecto**	insect
el **animal**	animal	el **invertebrado**	invertebrate
las **branquias**	branchiae	el **reptil**	reptile
la **característica**	characteristic	el **tipo**	type
el **cocodrilo**	crocodile	el **vertebrado**	vertebrate
la **fotografía**	photograph	la **zoología**	zoology
el **grupo**	group		

NOUNS

el **ave** bird, fowl
la **clase** kind, type
la **columna vertebral** spine
la **escama** scale
el **huevo** egg
la **lagartija** lizard
el **mamífero** mammal
el **pelo** hair
el **pez**[1] fish
el **pico** beak
la **pluma** feather
la **rana** frog
el **renacuajo** tadpole
la **serpiente** snake, serpent
la **tortuga** turtle
la **vida** life

VERBS

existir to exist
explicar to explain
nacer to be born
pertenecer to belong

ADJECTIVES

caliente hot
cubierto(-a) (de) covered (with)
frío(-a) cold
grande large, big
vivo(-a) alive

OTHER WORDS AND EXPRESSIONS

en forma de in the shape of
se divide is divided
si if

---

[1]When still in the water. Once caught, the word is *pescado*.

LET'S PRACTICE

Give the Spanish equivalent of the words in parentheses and read aloud.

1. La maestra .... explica la lección.   (*to them*)

2. La señorita Paz .... de los reptiles.   (*is talking to us*)

3. .... animales son mamíferos.   (*Those*)

4. Ángel dice que los peces son invertebrados. .... no es verdad.   (*That*)

5. ¿Las fotografías? Ella ....   (*brings them to me*)

6. Los niños .... un libro sobre las aves.   (*are reading*)

7. Ella .... que los renacuajos respiran por las branquias.   (*is telling him*)

8. ¿Usted necesita el libro de zoología? Yo puedo ....   (*lend it to you*)

9. .... animales son vertebrados y .... son invertebrados.

   (*These / those*)

10. ¿Las láminas de los anfibios? .... , Paquito.   (*I can give them to you*)

CONVERSATION

Answer the following questions based on the dialogue.

1. ¿Qué les está explicando la maestra a los niños?

   ....

2. ¿En cuántos grandes grupos se divide el reino animal?   (¿Cuáles son?)

   ....

3. ¿Qué tipo de animales son los insectos?

   ....

4. ¿Cuál es la característica de los invertebrados?

   ....

5. ¿A qué grupo pertenecen las aves, los reptiles y los peces?

   ....

6. ¿Dónde vive un anfibio en la primera parte de su vida?

   ....

7. ¿Cómo respiran los renacuajos?

  ....

8. ¿Qué le va a preguntar Diego a su mamá?

  ....

9. ¿Qué son las serpientes, las lagartijas, las tortugas y los cocodrilos?

  ....

10. ¿Qué animales tienen el cuerpo cubierto de plumas?

  ....

11. ¿Qué animales nacen vivos y cuáles nacen de huevos?

  ....

12. ¿Qué animales tienen el cuerpo cubierto de escamas?

  ....

Some additional questions:

13. ¿Sabe usted mucho de zoología?

  ....

14. Yo no sé qué son los anfibios.   ¿Puede usted explicármelo?

  ....

15. ¿Tiene usted peces de colores en su casa?

  ....

16. Necesito un libro de zoología.   ¿A quién se lo puedo pedir?

  ....

17. Si yo necesito láminas de animales.   ¿Puede usted prestármelas?

  ....

18. En la biblioteca de su escuela, ¿hay muchos libros sobre animales?

  ....

DIALOGUE COMPLETION

La señorita Rivera les hace preguntas a los alumnos sobre los animales.

MAESTRA   — ....

ROSITA   —Tienen sangre caliente y el cuerpo cubierto de pelo.

MAESTRA	— ....
AURORA	—No, señorita; no nacen de huevos; nacen vivos.
MAESTRA	— ....
PEDRO	—Son los animales que tienen columna vertebral.
MAESTRA	— ....
GUADALUPE	—Tienen el cuerpo cubierto de plumas y la boca en forma de pico.
MAESTRA	— ....
RAÚL	—No, señorita; no es un pez; es un anfibio.
MAESTRA	— ....
CARLOS	—No, tienen sangre fría, como los peces.

SITUATIONAL EXERCISES

What would you say in the following situations?

1. Tell your students that you are going to talk to them about the different kinds of animals that exist in the world.   Then talk to them about the characteristics of the following kinds of animals.
   a. mammals
   b. fish
   c. birds
   d. amphibians
2. Tell your students where they can get more books on animals.

YOU'RE ON YOUR OWN!

With a classmate, act out the following:

A teacher and a student discussing different kinds of animals

VOCABULARY EXPANSION (Optional)

More words to talk about animals:

A.   Animales domésticos:

el **caballo** horse
la **cabra** goat
el **conejo** rabbit
la **gallina** hen
el **gallo** rooster
el **gato** cat
la **oveja** sheep
el **pájaro** bird
el **pato** duck

el **pavo** turkey
el **perro** dog
la **vaca** cow

B.   Animales salvajes:

el **camello** camel
la **cebra** zebra
el **elefante** elephant
la **girafa** giraffe

el **hipopótamo** hippopotamus

el **león** lion

el **mono** monkey

el **tigre** tiger

la **cucaracha** cockroach

la **hormiga** ant

la **mariposa** butterfly

el **mosquito** mosquito

C. *Insectos:*

la **abeja** bee

la **araña** spider

la **avispa** wasp

D. *Otros animales invertebrados:*

el **cangrejo** crab

el **caracol** snail

la **langosta** lobster

Do you remember the words included in the Vocabulary Expansion?

Write the names of the following animals in the space provided.

1. ....

2. ....

3. ....

4. ....

5. ....

6. ....

7. ....

1. ....   4. ....
2. ....   5. ....
3. ....

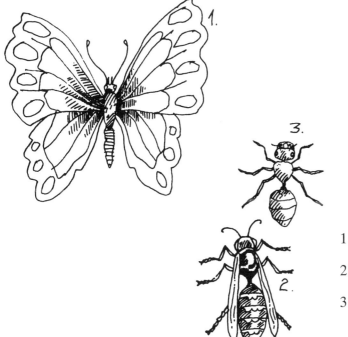

1. ....
2. ....
3. ....

Lesson 9

La señora Gómez habla con el maestro de su hijo

MAESTRO	—Siéntese, señora. Quiero hablar con Ud. porque Antonio tiene algunos problemas.
SRA. GÓMEZ	—Sí, sé que está atrasado en lectura.
MAESTRO	—Ahora está mejorando un poco, pero todavía no lee al nivel del grado.
SRA. GÓMEZ	—¿Está faltando a clase?
MAESTRO	—No, pero muchas veces llega tarde y se porta mal en clase.
SRA. GÓMEZ	—Yo no sé lo que le pasa...
MAESTRO	—Yo tampoco. Se pelea con los otros niños y les pega...
SRA. GÓMEZ	—Castíguelo... Déjelo en la escuela después de clase.
MAESTRO	—Ésa no es la solución. Trate de ayudarlo con la tarea y venga a observar la clase de vez en cuando.
SRA. GÓMEZ	—Yo no puedo porque trabajo, pero voy a decírselo a mi esposo.
MAESTRO	—Bueno... ¿El niño come bien? ¿Duerme bien?
SRA. GÓMEZ	—A veces no come nada por la mañana.
MAESTRO	—Dele un buen desayuno. Eso es muy importante.
SRA. GÓMEZ	—Muy bien. Mire, señor... yo creo que Antonio es inteligente...
MAESTRO	—Sí, tiene habilidad, pero, como no se esfuerza, está en el grupo de lectura más bajo.
SRA. GÓMEZ	—Yo creo que tambien tiene problemas con la vista.
MAESTRO	—Llévelo al oculista. Quizá necesita anteojos...
SRA. GÓMEZ	—Yo necesito cambiar los míos, así que puedo pedir turno para él también.
MAESTRO	—Gracias por venir.[1] ¡Ah! Ésta es la libreta de calificaciones de Antonio. Fírmela antes de irse,[1] por favor.

$$* \quad * \quad *$$

Mrs. Gomez Speaks with Her Son's Teacher

TEACHER:	Sit down, madam. I want to speak with you because Antonio has a few problems.
MRS. GOMEZ:	Yes, I know he's behind in reading.
TEACHER:	Now he's improving a little, but he still doesn't read at grade level.
MRS. GOMEZ:	Is he missing classes?
TEACHER:	No, but many times he's late and he misbehaves in class.
MRS. GOMEZ:	I don't know what's the matter with him . . .
TEACHER:	Neither do I. He fights with the other children and hits them . . .
MRS. GOMEZ:	Punish him . . . Leave him at school after class.
TEACHER:	That's not the solution. Try to help him with his homework and come to observe the class once in a while.
MRS. GOMEZ:	I can't because I work, but I'll tell my husband.

[1]In Spanish, the infinitive is used after a preposition.

TEACHER:	Okay . . . Does the child eat well? Does he sleep well?
MRS. GOMEZ:	Sometimes he doesn't eat anything in the morning.
TEACHER:	Give him a good breakfast. That's very important.
MRS. GOMEZ:	Very well. Look, sir . . . I think Antonio is intelligent . . .
TEACHER:	Yes, he has the ability, but, since he doesn't try, he's in the lowest reading group.
MRS. GOMEZ:	I think he also has problems with his eyes (sight).
TEACHER:	Take him to the ophthalmologist. Maybe he needs glasses . . .
MRS. GOMEZ:	I need to change mine, so I can make an appointment for him too.
TEACHER:	Thank you for coming. Oh! This is Antonio's report card. Sign it before you leave, please.

VOCABULARY

COGNATES

la **habilidad** ability   la **solución** solution

el, la **oculista** oculist

NOUNS

los **anteojos, lentes, espejuelos,** las **gafas**
  eyeglasses
el **desayuno** breakfast
el **grado** grade
el **nivel** level
la **vista** sight, eyesight

VERBS

ayudar to help
cambiar to change
castigar to punish
dejar to leave (behind)
esforzarse (o:ue) to try, to make an effort
observar to observe
pegar to hit
pelearse to fight
portarse to behave
tratar (de) to try

ADJECTIVES

atrasado(-a) behind
bajo(-a) low

OTHER WORDS AND EXPRESSIONS

al nivel del grado at grade level
así que so
de vez en cuando once in a while
faltar a clase to miss classes
lo que what
llegar tarde to be late
muchas veces many times
otro(-a) other, another
pedir turno to make an appointment
portarse mal to misbehave
quizá(s) maybe, perhaps
un poco a little

LET'S PRACTICE

A. **Tell a parent to do (or not to do) the following:**

1. Ayudar a su hijo con la tarea y no castigarlo.

  ....

2. Observar la clase.

  ....

3. Darle un buen desayuno al niño.

  ....

   4. Firmar la libreta de calificaciones.

   ....

   5. Sentarse.

   ....

   6. Ir a hablar con el director y decirle que su hijo tiene problemas.

   ....

   7. Pedirle turno al oculista para su hijo.

   ....

B. Tell your students to do (or not do to) the following:

   1. No dejar los libros en casa; traerlos todos los días.

   ....

   2. No pelearse con los otros niños y no pegarles.

   ....

   3. Portarse bien.

   ....

   4. No faltar a clase y no llegar tarde.

   ....

   5. Levantarse más temprano y hacer la tarea.

   ....

   6. No portarse mal en clase.

   ....

   7. Prestar atención.

   ....

CONVERSATION

Answer the following questions based on the dialogue.

   1. ¿Por qué quiere hablar el maestro con la señora Gómez?

   ....

2. ¿En qué está atrasado Antonio?

....

3. ¿Lee Antonio al nivel del grado?

....

4. ¿Antonio falta a clase o llega tarde?

....

5. ¿Cómo se porta Antonio en clase?

....

6. ¿Sabe la señora Gómez lo que le pasa a Antonio?

....

7. ¿Qué cree el maestro que debe hacer la señora Gómez?

....

8. ¿Qué debe hacer la señora Gómez de vez en cuando?

....

9. ¿Por qué está Antonio en el grupo de lectura más bajo?

....

10. ¿A dónde debe llevar la señora Gómez a su hijo y por qué?

....

Some additional questions:

11. ¿Necesita Ud. anteojos para leer?

....

12. ¿Tiene Ud. problemas con la vista?

....

13. ¿Castiga Ud. a sus estudiantes?

....

14. ¿Falta Ud. mucho a clase?

....

15. ¿Habla Ud. español de vez en cuando?

....

16. ¿Necesita Ud. cambiar su coche?

....

17. ¿Qué hace Ud. para mejorar en la clase de español?

....

18. Yo tengo mi libro de español. ¿Dónde está el suyo?

....

DIALOGUE COMPLETION

Using your imagination and the vocabulary learned in this lesson, complete the missing parts of this dialogue.

La señora Vargas viene a hablar con la maestra de su hija:

MAESTRA —Señora, tengo muchos problemas con Luisa.

SRA. VARGAS —¿ .... ?

MAESTRA —Sí, se porta muy mal. Y no hace la tarea.

SRA. VARGAS — ....

MAESTRA —Eso no es verdad. Ella tiene tarea todos los días.

SRA. VARGAS — ....

MAESTRA —Castigarla no es la solución. Debe ayudarla.

SRA. VARGAS — ....

MAESTRA —Sí, yo también creo que tiene problemas con la vista.

SRA. VARGAS — ....

MAESTRA —Llévela. Quizá necesita espejuelos.

SRA. VARGAS — ....

MAESTRA —Sí, señora. Su hija es inteligente, pero no se esfuerza por mejorar.

SRA. VARGAS — ....

MAESTRA —Sí, ayúdela con la tarea y dígale que debe estudiar más.

SRA. VARGAS — ....

MAESTRA —Sí, aquí está. Fírmela antes de irse, por favor.

SITUATIONAL EXERCISES

What would you say in the following situations?

1. Tell a parent to take his son to the ophthalmologist, because you think that he has a problem with his eyes and that maybe he needs glasses.
2. Tell a student that he has ability and that, if he makes an effort, he can improve.
3. A mother thinks she should punish her daughter for not studying. Tell her that that is not the solution, and suggest that she try to help her daughter with her homework.
4. Tell a parent that many times his son is late to class so he doesn't know what the other children are doing.
5. A father is worried about his son's progress in class. Tell him he's improving a little, but that he fights with the other children and hits them. Say that you don't know what's the matter with him.

YOU'RE ON YOUR OWN!

With a classmate, act out the following:

A parent and a teacher are discussing a child's progress and discipline problems. The teacher should make a few suggestions to improve the child's performance and behavior.

VOCABULARY EXPANSION (Optional)

Other things a teacher might need to say to a parent:

es urgente   it is urgent
está adelantado(-a)   is ahead of the class
está progresando   is progressing
interrumpe la clase   disturbs the class
no devuelve los libros   doesn't return books
no oye bien   is hard of hearing (doesn't hear well)
no se preocupe   don't worry

no se siente bien   isn't feeling well
¿Puede venir a buscar (recoger) a su hijo(-a)?
   Can you come to pick up your son (daughter)?
sea consistente   be consistent
tiene fiebre   has a fever
vomitó   he threw up

Do you remember the phrases included in the Vocabulary Expansion?

You need to say the following to the parents of some of your students.   How do you say it in Spanish?

A.   Your son

....

(Your daughter)

(.............................)

1. is hard of hearing.

....

2. does not return books.

....

3. is progressing.

....

4. disturbs the class.

....

5. is ahead (of the class).

....

6. isn't feeling well.

....

7. has a temperature.

....

8. threw up.

....

B.

1. It is urgent.

....

2. Can you come to pick up your daughter (son)?

....

3. Don't worry.

....

4. Be consistent.

....

71

Lesson 10

Una excursión al jardín botánico

El señor Ochoa y la señora Pérez llevan a sus alumnos de segundo y tercer grado al jardín botánico para enseñarles algo acerca de las plantas.

SR. OCHOA	—Bájense del ómnibus y pónganse en fila. No se separen de nosotros.
SRA. PÉREZ	—Caminen de dos en dos y tómense de las manos.
SR. OCHOA	—Aquí vamos a ver plantas de distintos países y climas.
PACO	—Aquí hay un árbol de Cuba. ¡Qué alto es!
SRA. PÉREZ	—Los árboles son las plantas más grandes. ¿Quién sabe cuáles son las partes de una planta?
AURORA	—La raíz, el tallo y las hojas.
CARLOS	—¡Y las flores y los frutos! Yo tengo un naranjo en mi patio. Me lo dio mi tío.
SRA. PÉREZ	—¿Dónde está Raquel?
EVA	—Fue al baño. Ahí viene ya.
SR. OCHOA	—¿Por qué son importantes los árboles?
RAMÓN	—Porque nos dan madera para hacer muebles.
SR. OCHOA	—Con la madera también se hace papel.
SRA. PÉREZ	—¿Cómo se alimentan las plantas? ¿Alguien lo sabe?
RAÚL	—¿Con agua?
SRA. PÉREZ	—El agua ayuda, pero la planta toma parte de sus alimentos de la tierra…
ELENA	—¿Y eso sube por el tronco?
SRA. PÉREZ	—Sí, y las hojas usan la luz del sol para transformarlo en alimento para la planta.
JOSÉ	—Yo quiero ir a ver los cactus. El año pasado fuimos a Arizona y vi muchos allí.
SR. OCHOA	—Eso es porque los cactus son plantas del desierto.
TERESA	—Yo encontré una semilla y alguien me la quitó. ¿Quién fue?
SARA	—¡Fue Jorge!

Los niños pasaron toda la mañana en el jardín botánico y aprendieron mucho. Ahora tienen que volver a la escuela.

SRA. PÉREZ	—Apúrense porque está empezando a lloviznar.
SR. OCHOA	—Vamos por aquí. Súbanse al ómnibus y siéntense.

✳   ✳   ✳

A Field Trip to the Botanical Gardens

Mr. Ochoa and Mrs. Perez take their second and third grade students to the botanical gardens to teach them something about plants.

MR. OCHOA:	Get off the bus and stand in line. Stay with us (don't get separated from us).
MRS. PEREZ:	Walk in pairs and hold hands.
MR. OCHOA:	Here we're going to see plants from different countries and climates.
PACO:	Here (there) is a tree from Cuba. How tall it is!

MRS. PEREZ:	Trees are the largest plants. Who knows what the parts of a plant are?
AURORA:	The root, the stem, and the leaves.
CARLOS:	And the flowers and the fruit! I have an orange tree in my backyard. My uncle gave it to me.
MRS. PEREZ:	Where's Raquel?
EVA:	She went to the bathroom. She's coming now.
MR. OCHOA:	Why are trees important?
RAMON:	Because they give us wood to make furniture.
MR. OCHOA:	With wood they also make paper.
MRS. PEREZ:	How do plants get nourishment? Does anybody know?
RAUL:	With water?
MRS. PEREZ:	Water helps, but the plant takes part of its nourishment from the soil . . .
ELENA	And that goes up the trunk?
MRS. PEREZ:	Yes, and the leaves use the sunlight to transform it into nourishment for the plant.
JOSE:	I want to go see the cacti. Last year we went to Arizona and I saw many there.
MR. OCHOA:	That's because cacti are desert plants.
TERESA:	I found a seed and someone took it away from me. Who was it?
SARA:	It was Jorge!

The children spent the whole morning at the botanical gardens and they learned a great deal. Now they have to go back to school.

MRS. PEREZ:	Hurry up because it's beginning to drizzle.
MR. OCHOA:	Let's go this way. Get on the bus and sit down.

VOCABULARY

COGNATES

el **cactus** cactus	la **planta** plant
el **desierto** desert	

NOUNS

el **alimento** nourishment, food, nutrient
el **árbol** tree
la **excursión** field trip
la **fila** line
la **flor** flower
el **fruto** fruit
la **hoja** leaf
el **jardín** garden
el **jardín botánico** botanical gardens
la **luz** light
la **luz del sol** sunlight
el **naranjo** orange tree
el **patio** backyard
la **raíz** root
la **semilla** seed
el **sol** sun
el **tallo** stem
la **tierra** soil, earth
el **tronco** (tree) trunk

VERBS

alimentar(se) to feed, to nourish, to get
  nourishment

apurarse to hurry up
bajar(se) to get off
caminar to walk
encontrar (o:ue) to find
enseñar to teach
lloviznar to drizzle
pasar to spend (time)
separar(se) to separate, to get separated
subir(se) to get on
transformar to turn into, to transform

OTHER WORDS AND EXPRESSIONS

acerca de about
ahí there
ahí viene ya she's coming now
caminen de dos en dos walk in pairs
no se separen de nosotros stay with us (don't
  get separated from us)
ponerse en fila to stand in line
por aquí this way
tómense de las manos hold hands

LET'S PRACTICE!

Change the following to the preterit:

1. Los niños *van* de excursión.

   ....

2. Los *llevan* al jardín botánico.

   ....

3. Allí *ven* muchas plantas.

   ....

4. Les *damos* plantas para el patio.

   ....

5. *Voy* al baño.

   ....

6. No *te separas* de nosotros.

   ....

7. *Caminamos* de dos en dos.

   ....

8. *Aprende* mucho acerca de las plantas.

   ....

9. ¿Tú me *escribes*?

   ....

10. Ellos *son* mis alumnos.

    ....

CONVERSATION

Answer the following questions based on the dialogue.

1. ¿A dónde llevan los maestros a los niños?

   ....

2. ¿Para qué los llevan al jardín botánico?

   ....

3. ¿Cómo deben caminar los niños?

....

4. ¿Qué van a ver los niños en el jardín botánico?

....

5. ¿Cuáles son las partes de una planta?

....

6. Carlos tiene un naranjo.   ¿Quién se lo dio?

....

7. ¿A dónde fue Raquel?

....

8. ¿Qué se hace con la madera?

....

9. ¿De dónde toma la planta parte de sus alimentos?

....

10. ¿Quién encontró una semilla?

....

11. ¿Quién se la quitó?

....

12. ¿Por qué deben apurarse los niños?

....

Some additional questions:

13. ¿Llevó Ud. a sus alumnos al jardín botánico?

....

14. ¿Qué grado enseñó Ud. el año pasado?

....

15. ¿Fue Ud. al desierto el verano pasado?

....

16. ¿Tiene Ud. árboles en su patio?

....

17. ¿Va en coche a la escuela o prefiere caminar?

    ....

18. ¿Sus alumnos se ponen en fila antes de entrar en la clase?

    ....

19. ¿Cuántas horas pasa Ud. en la escuela?

    ....

20. ¿Tiene Ud. muchas flores en su jardín?

    ....

DIALOGUE COMPLETION

Using your imagination and the vocabulary learned in this lesson, fill in the missing parts of this dialogue.

La señorita Soto y sus alumnos están en el jardín botánico.

MAESTRA —...

JORGE —La raíz, el tallo, las hojas, las flores y los frutos.

MAESTRA —...

MARÍA —Porque nos dan madera.

MAESTRA —...

CARLOS —Toma parte de sus alimentos de la tierra.

MAESTRA —...

JORGE —Hay muchos cactus en el desierto.

MAESTRA —...

EVA —Ahora queremos ir a ver las flores.

SUSANA —¡Señorita! ¡Está empezando a lloviznar!

MAESTRA —...

SITUATIONAL EXERCISES

What would you say in the following situations?

1. You are explaining how a tree gets its nourishment. Tell your students that a tree takes part of its food from the soil, and that goes up the trunk. Add that the leaves use the sunlight to turn it into food.

2. Comment that it is beginning to drizzle. Tell your students to hurry up and get on the bus.
3. Your students are on a field trip. Tell them to get off the bus, walk in pairs and hold hands.
4. Another teacher asks you where Antonio is. Tell her that he went to the bathroom and that he's coming now.

YOU'RE ON YOUR OWN!

With a classmate, act out the following situations:

1. A teacher and a student talking about plants
2. Two teachers giving instructions to students during a field trip

VOCABULARY EXPANSION (Optional)

Algunas flores:

la **camelia** camelia
el **clavel** carnation
la **margarita** daisy
la **orquídea** orchid
el **pensamiento** pansy
la **rosa** rose
la **violeta** violet

Algunas frutas:

la **cereza** cherry
la **fresa** strawberry
el **limón** lemon
la **manzana** apple
la **naranja** orange
la **pera** pear
el **plátano**, la **banana** banana
la **toronja** grapefruit
la **uva** grape

Algunos vegetales:

el **ají** green pepper
el **ajo** garlic
el **apio** celery
la **cebolla** onion
la **lechuga** lettuce
la **papa, patata** potato
el **repollo,** la **col** cabbage
la **zanahoria** carrot

Do you remember the words included in the Vocabulary Expansion?

Write the names of the flower, vegetable or fruit in the spaces provided:

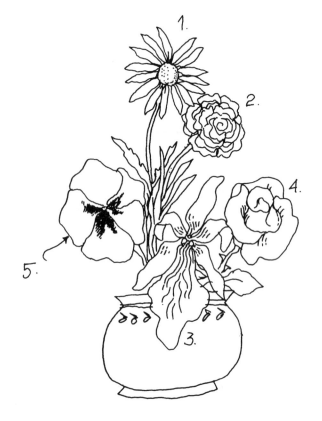

1. ....
2. ....
3. ....
4. ....
5. ....

78

1. ....

2. ....

3. ....

4. ....

5. ....

6. ....

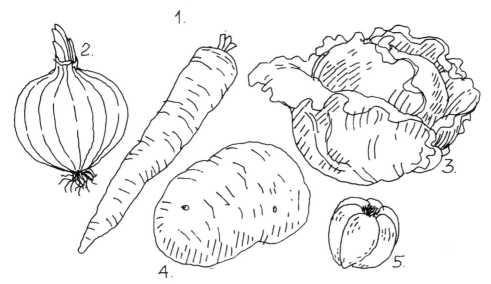

1. ....

2. ....

3. ....

4. ....

5. ....

LESSONS 6–10   # VOCABULARY REVIEW

A. Circle the word or phrase that does not belong in each group.

1. articulación, coyuntura, intestino
2. cráneo, pulmones, cerebro
3. hueso, esqueleto, microbio
4. sangre, glóbulos rojos, tráquea
5. timbre, rodilla, codo
6. bronquios, vasos capilares, pulmones
7. flor, fruto, patio
8. estómago, cabeza, digestión
9. anteojos, jardín, espejuelos
10. piel, pigmento, sol
11. músculo, tronco, tallo
12. enseñar, llover, lloviznar
13. rana, ave, renacuajo
14. caliente, grande, frío
15. pelo, cáctus, desierto
16. vena, nivel, arteria

B. Circle the appropriate word or phrase that completes each of the following sentences.

1. Caminen de dos en dos y tómense (del pelo, de la cabeza, de las manos).
2. El corazón es el órgano que (opera, envía, nombra) la sangre a todo el cuerpo.
3. Se porta muy mal. Voy a (pensarlo, castigarlo, sostenerlo).
4. Las plantas toman su alimento de (la tierra, la clase, la unión).
5. Vamos a comer. Es la hora (de llegar tarde, de levantar la mano, del almuerzo).
6. Está muy atrasado porque (falta mucho a clase, se pone en fila, ahí viene ya).
7. La lagartija, el cocodrilo y la tortuga pertenecen al grupo de los (peces, mamíferos, reptiles).
8. La piel protege el cuerpo de (la raíz, la hoja, los microbios).
9. No mejora porque no (pelea, se esfuerza, deja).
10. Las aves (existen, explican, nacen) de huevos.
11. Una lagartija pertenece al reino (mineral, animal, vegetal).
12. Voy a pegar esta (fotografía, persona, ropa) en mi cuaderno.
13. Si no ve bien, tiene que (ir, ayudar, transformar) al frente de la clase.
14. No trabaja al nivel del grado, así que está (oscuro, protegido, atrasado).
15. Las plantas necesitan la luz del (sol, elemento, pico).
16. Las aves tienen el cuerpo cubierto de (escamas, pelos, plumas).

17. En la clase de zoología, la maestra nos (movió, encontró, enseñó) las características de varios tipos de animales.

18. Éste es el problema. La (solución, semilla, habilidad) depende de Ud.

19. A la hora de almorzar, no deben (apurarse, separarse, sentarse) de nosotros.

20. Solamente lo veo de vez en (como, cuando, otro).

C.   Match the items in column *A* with those in column *B*.

A	*B*
1. ¿Las aves nacen vivas?	a. De plantas
2. ¿Estás listo?	b. Los glóbulos blancos
3. ¿De qué sufre?	c. En tres
4. ¿Qué cantidad necesitas?	d. Quizás estudian
5. ¿De qué trata la lección?	e. Coyuntura
6. ¿De qué se alimenta?	f. Los niños se están peleando.
7. ¿Cómo se llama la unión de dos huesos?	g. Dos días
8. ¿En cuántas partes se divide?	h. Todavía no
9. ¿Qué animales tienen la boca en forma de pico?	i. De huesos
10. ¿Qué es lo que debemos observar?	j. De los mamíferos
11. ¿Cuánto tiempo va a pasar aquí?	k. Por aquí
12. ¿Cómo se llama la armazón del cuerpo?	l. Veinte o treinta
13. ¿Qué hacen antes de comer?	m. Las aves
14. ¿Por dónde vamos?	n. No, nacen de huevos
15. ¿Qué pasa aquí?	o. Esqueleto
16. ¿De qué está formado el esqueleto?	p. Del corazón
17. ¿Quieres cambiarlo?	q. Sí, aprendieron mucho acerca de las plantas.
18. ¿Les enseñaste algo?	r. No, me gusta mucho.

D.   Crucigrama

HORIZONTAL

2. Debemos ____ bien la comida antes de tragarla.

4. lentes

5. primera comida del día

7. Las plaquetas sirven para ____ la sangre.

8. Los peces respiran por ____ .

10. Los ____ son las plantas más grandes.

11. La naranja es el fruto del ____ .

14. Vamos de excursión al jardín ____ .

16. Los pulmones forman parte del aparato ____ .

20. Suena el ____ para la salida.

21. El esqueleto es la ____ del cuerpo.

22. Necesitamos ____ para respirar.

25. El corazón es parte del aparato ____ .

27. opuesto de mucho: un ____

28. opuesto de **sin**

VERTICAL

1. opuesto de bajarse
3. Los peces tienen el cuerpo cubierto de _____ .
6. Tengo problemas con la vista. Voy a pedirle turno al _____ .
8. opuesto de **alto**
9. La rana es un _____ .
12. diferente
13. Los vertebrados tienen columna _____ .
15. Los pulmones toman el oxígeno para _____ la sangre.

17. La _____ es un reptil.
18. Los insectos son animales _____ .
19. Estudiamos el sistema nervioso en la clase de _____ .
23. Pepito está en el tercer _____ .
24. La _____ cubre todo nuestro cuerpo.
26. opuesto de nada

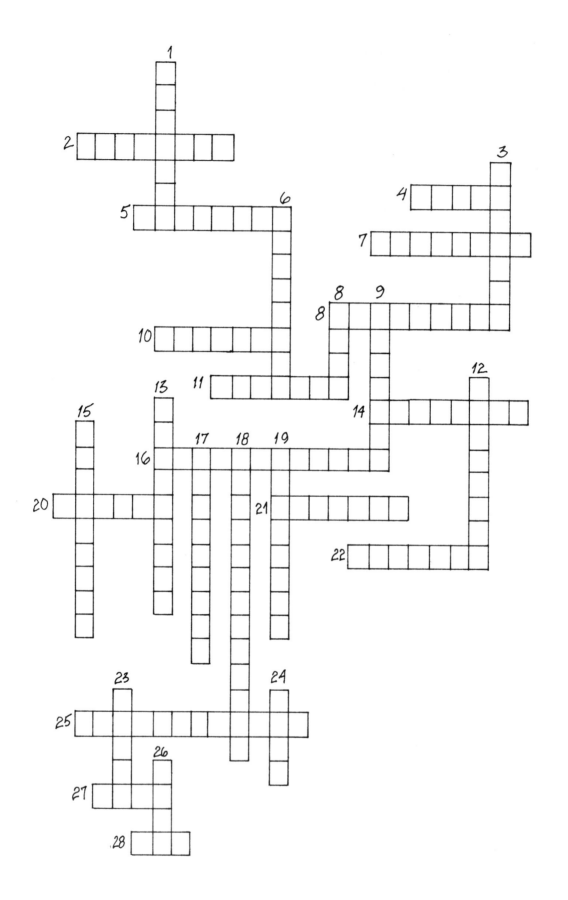

Lesson 11

Algunas reglas de ortografía

Los alumnos de la Srta. Suárez llevan dos semanas preparándose para un concurso de ortografía.

MAESTRA —Díganme las reglas que debemos recordar sobre el uso de la vocal *i* antes de la vocal *e,* o la *e* antes de la *i.* ¿Ramón?

RAMÓN —La primera es que generalmente se escribe *i* antes de *e.*

DORA —Sí, excepto después de la letra *ce.*

MAESTRA —¿Es ésa la única excepción? ¿Miguel?

MIGUEL —También cuando se pronuncia *ei,* como en la palabra *eight.*

MAESTRA —¿Y qué pasa cuando la combinación está precedida por el sonido *sh?*

HILDA —Entonces se escribe la *i* antes de la *e,* aunque hay excepciones...

DIEGO —Señorita, ¿cómo se escribe "*running*"?

MAESTRA —¡Diego! Hace dos semanas que explico las reglas de ortografía, ¿y todavía me lo preguntas?

MÓNICA —¡Búscala en el diccionario!

DIEGO —Yo no traje el mío. ¿De quién es éste que está aquí?

SILVIA —Es mío, pero puedes usarlo.

MAESTRA —No es necesario. A ver... ¿Quién sabe cuándo debemos doblar la consonante final antes de un sufijo?

DAVID —Cuando la palabra termina en una sola consonante, precedida por una sola vocal.

ELVIRA —Eso sólo no basta. Debe ser una palabra de una sola sílaba, o debe estar acentuada en la última sílaba.

RITA —Y además, el sufijo debe comenzar con una vocal.

MAESTRA —Dime, Hugo, ¿qué ocurre cuando el acento pasa de la última sílaba a otra?

HUGO —Entonces no se dobla la consonante.

MAESTRA —¡Muy bien! Hay otras reglas sobre esto. Estúdienlas para mañana. Estudien también cómo se forman los plurales, y el pasado de los verbos regulares.

SANDRA —Maestra, yo ya hice los ejercicios de los verbos irregulares. Ud. dijo que iba a revisarlos hoy...

MAESTRA —No, voy a corregirlos mañana. No todos los trajeron hoy.

SANDRA —Cuando yo no hacía mi tarea, la otra maestra siempre me castigaba...

* * *

Some Spelling Rules

Miss Suarez's students have been preparing for a spelling bee for two weeks.

TEACHER: Tell me the rules that we must remember about the use of the vowel *i* before the vowel *e,* or the *e* before the *i.* Ramon?

RAMON: The first one is that generally *i* comes before *e* (one spells *i* before *e*).

DORA: Yes, except after the letter *c.*

TEACHER: Is that the only exception? Miguel?

MIGUEL: Also when it's pronounced *ei,* as in the word *eight.*

TEACHER:	And what happens when the combination is preceded by the *sh* sound?
HILDA:	Then the *i* comes before the *e*, although there are exceptions . . .
DIEGO:	Teacher, how does one spell '*running*'?
TEACHER:	Diego! I have been explaining the spelling rules for two weeks, and you're still asking me?
MONICA:	Look it up in the dictionary!
DIEGO:	I didn't bring mine. Whose is this one here?
SILVIA:	It's mine, but you may use it.
TEACHER:	It's not necessary. Let's see . . . Who knows when we must double the final consonant before a suffix?
DAVID:	When a word ends in a single consonant, preceded by a single vowel.
ELVIRA:	That alone is not enough. It must be a one-syllable word, or it must be stressed on the last syllable.
RITA:	And furthermore, the suffix must start with a vowel.
TEACHER:	Tell me, Hugo, what happens when the stress goes from the last syllable to another one?
HUGO:	Then the consonant is not doubled.
TEACHER:	Very good! There are other rules about this. Study them for tomorrow. Study also how the plurals are formed and the past tense of regular verbs.
SANDRA:	Teacher, I already did the exercise on irregular verbs. You said you were going to check them today . . .
TEACHER:	No, I'm going to correct them tomorrow. Not everybody brought them today.
SANDRA:	When I didn't do my homework, the other teacher used to punish me . . .

VOCABULARY

COGNATES

la **combinación** combination	**necesario(-a)** necessary
la **consonante** consonant	el **plural** plural
la **excepción** exception	**precedido(-a)** preceded
excepto except	**regular** regular
final final	la **sílaba** syllable
generalmente generally	el **sufijo** suffix
irregular irregular	el **uso** use

NOUNS

el **acento** stress
el **concurso** contest
el **concurso de ortografía** spelling bee
el **pasado** past
la **regla** rule
el **sonido** sound
la **vocal** vowel

VERBS

bastar to be enough
corregir (e:i) to correct
doblar to double
formar to form
ocurrir to happen
pasar to pass, to go
prepararse to prepare oneself, to get ready
pronunciar to pronounce
revisar to check

ADJECTIVES

acentuado(-a) accented
último(-a) last

OTHER WORDS AND EXPRESSIONS

a ver... let's see . . .
además besides, furthermore
aunque although
como like, as
entonces then, in that case
eso solo that by itself
está precedido(-a) por is preceded by
se escribe is written
sobre about
sólo only
todavía still
una sola a single
único(-a) only
usted iba a... you were going to . . .

LET'S PRACTICE

A.   Tell for how long each action has been going on.   Use *hace…que*.

Modelo: Roberto empezó a estudiar a las seis.   Son las ocho.
         Hace dos horas que Roberto estudia.

1. Ellos empezaron a prepararse para el concurso el lunes.   Hoy es jueves.

....

2. Empecé a corregir los exámenes a las doce.   Ahora son las cinco.

....

3. Empecé a revisar los ejercicios a las once.   Son las seis y media.

....

4. Empezaste tu tarea viernes.   Hoy es lunes.

....

B.   Change the following sentences, first to the preterit and then to the imperfect.

1. *Voy* aunque *llueve*.

....

....

2. No *es* eso sólo.

....

....

3. Aquí no *ocurre* nada.

....

....

4. Eso no *basta*.

....

....

5. A ver… ¿quién *viene*?

....

....

6. Les *traen* el libro de ortografía.

  ....

  ....

7. Entonces no *hacemos* nada.

  ....

  ....

8. *Tengo* que estudiar las excepciones.

  ....

  ....

9. No *puede* castigarlo.

  ....

  ....

10. No *dice* nada.

  ....

  ....

CONVERSATION

Answer the following questions based on the dialogue.

1. ¿Cuánto tiempo hace que los alumnos se preparan para el concurso de ortografía?

  ....

2. ¿Se escribe *i* antes de *e* después de la letra *ce*?

  ....

3. ¿Cuánto tiempo lleva la maestra explicando las reglas de ortografía?

  ....

4. ¿De quién es el diccionario?

  ....

5. ¿Por qué se dobla la consonante *-n* en la palabra "*running*"?

  ....

  ....

6. ¿Qué deben estudiar los niños para mañana?

  ....

7. ¿Quién ya hizo el ejercicio de los verbos irregulares?

  ....

8. ¿Por qué no va a corregir la maestra los ejercicios hoy?

  ....

9. ¿Qué hacía la maestra de Sandra cuando la niña no hacía la tarea?

  ....

Some additional questions:

10. ¿Cómo se escribe su nombre?

  ....

11. ¿Cuánto tiempo hace que Ud. enseña?

  ....

12. ¿Es fácil o difícil pronunciar su apellido?

  ....

13. En la palabra "formar", ¿qué sílaba va acentuada?

  ....

14. ¿Ud. iba a estudiar con sus amigos?

  ....

15. Para aprender a hablar bien el español, ¿basta con saber reglas de gramática?

  ....

16. ¿Hizo Ud. todos los ejercicios de la lección diez?

  ....

17. ¿Revisa Ud. la tarea de sus alumnos todos los días?

  ....

18. ¿A qué escuela iba Ud. cuando era niño(-a)?

  ....

19. ¿Dónde vivía Ud. cuando era niño(-a)?

  ....

20. Cuando Ud. era alumno(a), ¿sabía todas las reglas de ortografía?

  ....

DIALOGUE COMPLETION

Using your imagination and the vocabulary learned in this lesson, fill in the missing parts of the dialogue.

El señor García repasa con sus alumnos algunas reglas de ortografía.

MAESTRO —..

PEDRO —Sí, excepto después de la letra *ce*.

MAESTRO —..

CARMEN —No, no es la única excepción. Hay otras además de ésa.

MAESTRO —..

ELENA —Cuando la combinación está precedida por el sonido *sh*.

TERESA —Señor, ¿por qué se dobla la *-n* en la palabra *running*?

MAESTRO —..

....

DIEGO —Señor, en la palabra "*careless*" ¿cuál es el sufijo?

MAESTRO —..

CARLOTA —¿Qué ocurre cuando el acento pasa de la última sílaba a otra?

MAESTRO —..

RITA —¿Tenemos que estudiar cómo se forman los plurales?

MAESTRO —..

RAÚL —¿El pasado de los verbos irregulares también?

MAESTRO —..

CARMEN —Yo todavía no entiendo lo que Ud. explicó ayer...

MAESTRO —..

CARMEN —Yo estudio... pero es muy difícil.

TERESA —¿Es necesario traer el diccionario mañana?

MAESTRO —..

SITUATIONAL EXERCISES

What would you say in the following situations?

1. You are speaking about a few grammar rules. Explain the following:
   a. There are some rules we must remember about the use of the vowel *-i* before the vowel *-e* or *-e* before *-i*.

90

   b. Generally, when the combination *ei* is preceded by the sound "*sh*", *-i* comes before *-e*, although there are some exceptions.

   c. The last consonant is doubled before a suffix when:

      (1) the word ends in a single consonant, preceded by a single vowel.

      (2) it is a one-syllable word or the stress is on the last syllable.

      (3) the suffix begins with a vowel.

   d. When the stress goes from the last syllable to another, the last consonant is not doubled.

2. Tell a student to come early tomorrow and bring his or her homework.

YOU'RE ON YOUR OWN!

With a classmate, act out the following:

A teacher trying to explain some spelling rules to a student after class

VOCABULARY EXPANSION

A. *Punctuation marks:*

,	coma	;	punto y coma
.	punto	:	dos puntos
" "	comillas	¿ ?	signos de interrogación
¡ !	signos de admiración	( )	paréntesis
/ /	barras	[ ]	corchetes
'	apóstrofe	-	guión

B. *Other words and phrases related to spelling:*

agregar, añadir   to add
el **alfabeto, abecedario**   alphabet
la **contracción**   contraction
el **dictado**   dictation
mudo(-a), sin sonido   silent

el **prefijo**   prefix
separar en sílabas   to separate into syllables
singular   singular

Do you remember the words and phrases included in the Vocabulary Expansion?

A.   Write the names of the following puncutation marks:

    1. -

    2. ;

    3. / /

    4. ,

    5. ¿ ?

    6. '

    7. :

    8. ( )

    9. .

   10. ¡ !

   11. [ ]

   12. " "

B.   Complete the following sentences appropriately.

    1. El .... tiene 26 letras.

    2. La palabra *isn't* es una ....

    3. En la palabra "hola", la letra *h* es ....

    4. No es plural; es ....

5. Para formar el plural de "letra", es necesario .... una -s.

6. En la palabra *undress,* la sílaba *un* es un ....

7. Para formar el plural de "lápiz", se .... la -z por una -c, y se

   .... -es.

8. Voy a .... la palabra "precedido". "pre-ce-di-do."

9. Escriban lo que digo. Es un ....

Lesson 12

Una clase de historia

Hoy los estudiantes de la señora López están hablando de algunos de los acontecimientos más importantes en la historia de los Estados Unidos.

MAESTRA —¿Quién descubrió América?

JOSÉ —La descubrió Cristóbal Colón en el año 1492.

SILVIA —Pero Colón nunca vino a los Estados Unidos, ¿verdad?

MAESTRA —No, los que colonizaron este país fueron principalmente los ingleses, pero hubo gente de otras nacionalidades.

JOSÉ —¿De qué países eran?

MAESTRA —De España, Francia, Holanda…

MARTA —Pero los peregrinos que llegaron en el Mayflower eran ingleses, ¿no?

MAESTRA —Sí, mucha gente vino de Inglaterra para librarse de la persecución religiosa.

CARLOS —¿Pero cuándo se formaron los Estados Unidos?

MAESTRA —En el siglo XVII y a principios del XVIII, de un grupo de colonias inglesas que estaban establecidas en la costa este.

EDUARDO —¿Por qué quería venir la gente a América?

MAESTRA —Porque sabía que había mucha tierra cultivable y barata. ¿Quién sabe qué pasó en el año 1776?

LUISA —Se declaró la independencia de los Estados Unidos.

MAESTRA —¿Quién fue el primer presidente y en qué año lo eligieron?

MARIO —Jorge Washington. Lo eligieron en 1778. Ésas fueron las primeras elecciones bajo la constitución.

MAESTRA —Muy bien. ¿Cuándo comenzó la Guerra Civil y cuánto tiempo duró?

ANTONIO —Comenzó en 1861 y duró cuatro años.

MAESTRA —¿Quién era el presidente en esa época?

EVA —Abraham Lincoln. Él abolió la esclavitud.

MAESTRA —Muy bien. Para mañana, lean la página 231 del libro de historia.

Esta es parte de la información que aparece en la página 231:

> A fines del siglo XIX y principios del XX, los Estados Unidos eran ya una potencia.
> En 1914 estalló la primera guerra mundial. Los norteamericanos trataron de mantenerse neutrales, pero entraron en la guerra en 1917.
> Durante la década de los años XX hubo prosperidad en los Estados Unidos, pero en 1929 comenzó la depresión.
> En 1939 comenzó la segunda guerra mundial. Los Estados Unidos se mantuvieron neutrales hasta el año 1941, cuando los japoneses bombardearon Pearl Harbor y el Congreso declaró guerra contra el Japón.
> La guerra terminó en 1945.

*   *   *

A History Class

Today Mrs. Lopez's students are talking about some of the most important events in the history of the United States.

TEACHER:	Who discovered America?
JOSE:	Christopher Columbus discovered it in the year 1492.
SILVIA:	But Columbus never came to the United States, right?
TEACHER:	No, the ones who colonized this country were mainly the English, but there were people of other nationalities.
JOSE:	From which countries were they?
TEACHER:	From Spain, France, Holland . . .
MARTA:	But the pilgrims that arrived on the Mayflower were English, weren't they?
TEACHER:	Yes, many people came from England to be free from religious persecution.
CARLOS:	But when were the United States established?
TEACHER:	In the 17th century and at the beginning of the 18th (century), from a group of English colonies which were established on the East coast.
EDUARDO:	Why did people want to come to America?
TEACHER:	Because they knew that there was a lot of cheap farmland. Who knows what happened in the year 1776?
LUISA:	The independence of the United States was declared.
TEACHER:	Who was the first president and in what year was he elected?
MARIO:	George Washington. He was elected in 1778. Those were the first elections under the constitution.
TEACHER:	Very good. When did the Civil War start and how long did it last?
ANTONIO:	It started in 1861 and it lasted four years.
TEACHER:	Who was the president at that time?
EVA:	Abraham Lincoln. He abolished slavery.
TEACHER:	Very good. For tomorrow, read page 231 in your history book.

This is part of the information that appears on page 231:

At the end of the 19th century and at the beginning of the 20th (century), the United States were already a power.

In 1914, the first world war broke out.   The Americans tried to be neutral, but they entered the war in 1917.

During the decade of the twenties there was prosperity in the United States, but in 1929 the depression started.

In 1939 the second world war started.   The United States were neutral until the year 1941, when the Japanese bombarded Pearl Harbor and Congress declared war against Japan.

The war ended in 1945.

94

VOCABULARY

COGNATES

civil civil	la **historia** history
la **colonia** colony	**Holanda** Holland
el **congreso** congress	**Japón** Japan
la **constitución** constitution	el, la **japonés(-esa)** Japanese
la **década** decade	**neutral** neutral
la **depresión** depression	la **persecución** persecution
la **elección** election	el, la **presidente(-a)** president
establecido(-a) established	la **prosperidad** prosperity
Francia France	**religioso(-a)** religious

NOUNS

el **acontecimiento** event
la **costa** coast
la **esclavitud** slavery
España Spain
la **gente** people
la **guerra** war
Inglaterra England
el, la **peregrino(-a)** pilgrim
la **potencia** power
el **siglo** century
la **tierra** land

VERBS

abolir to abolish
aparecer to appear
bombardear to bombard
colonizar to colonize
declarar to declare
descubrir to discover
durar to last
elegir (e:i) to elect, to choose
entrar (en) to enter

librarse (de) to be (become) free (from)
mantener(se) (*conj. like* **tener**) to keep
  (oneself), to maintain (oneself)

ADJECTIVES

barato(-a) inexpensive, cheap
mundial world, world-wide

OTHER WORDS AND EXPRESSIONS

a fines de at the end of
a principios de at the beginning of
bajo under
contra against
durante during
en esa época at that time
estalló la guerra the war started
formarse to be established
había there was, there were (imperfect)
hubo there was, there were (preterit)
los (las) que the ones who
principalmente mainly
tierra cultivable farmland

LET'S PRACTICE

Give the Spanish equivalent of the words in parentheses.

1. Yo .... a Carlos en Francia cuando .... quince años.

   (*met / I was*)

2. Lincoln .... la esclavitud en el siglo XIX. (*abolished*)

3. ¿Quién .... presidente en esa época?   (*was*)

4. En esa época la gente .... venir a América porque .... mucha tierra cultivable y barata.   (*wanted / there was*)

5. Nosotros .... principalmente los acontecimientos más importantes.   (*were studying*)

6. Las clases de historia .... dos horas.   (*used to last*)

7. Yo .... que ellos .... de Inglaterra.   Lo .... ayer.   (*didn't know / were / found out*)

8. Ella .... sola a Holanda el año pasado porque Mario .... ir con ella.   (*went / refused*)

CONVERSATION

Answer the following questions based on the dialogue.

1. ¿Quién descubrió América?   (¿En qué año?)

....

2. ¿Quiénes colonizaron este país?

....

3. ¿De qué nacionalidad eran los peregrinos que llegaron en el Mayflower?

....

4. ¿Qué hizo mucha gente de Inglaterra para librarse de la persecución religiosa?

....

5. ¿En qué año se declaró la independencia de los Estados Unidos?

....

6. ¿En qué año eligieron presidente a Jorge Washington?

....

7. ¿Cuándo comenzó la Guerra Civil y cuánto tiempo duró?

....

8. ¿En qué año estalló la primera guerra mundial?

....

9. ¿Pudieron los norteamericanos mantenerse neutrales en la primera guerra mundial?

....

96

10. ¿En qué año comenzó la depresión?

....

11. ¿En qué año bombardearon los japoneses Pearl Harbor?

....

12. ¿En qué año terminó la segunda guerra mundial?

....

Some additional questions:

13. ¿Vive Ud. más cerca de la costa del Atlántico o la costa del Pacífico?

....

14. ¿Quién era presidente cuando Ud. nació?

....

15. ¿Fue Ud. a España alguna vez? ¿Cuándo?

....

16. ¿Participa Ud. en todas las elecciones?

....

17. ¿Qué estaba haciendo Ud. durante la década de los setenta?

....

18. ¿Hubo alguna vez persecución religiosa en este país?

....

19. ¿Sabe Ud. quiénes escribieron la constitución de los Estados Unidos?

....

20. ¿Qué páginas tienen que estudiar Uds. para la próxima clase de español?

....

DIALOGUE COMPLETION

Using your imagination and the vocabulary you have learned in this lesson, fill in the missing parts of the following dialogue.

Hoy los estudiantes tienen un repaso de historia:

MAESTRA   —¿De qué países eran los que colonizaron los Estados Unidos?

ROSA   —...

MAESTRA —¿Dónde estaban establecidas las colonias inglesas de que se formaron los Estados Unidos?

ANA —..

MAESTRA —¿A quién eligieron presidente en las primeras elecciones?

CARLOS —..

MAESTRA —¿Cuántos años duró la primera guerra mundial?

RAÚL —..

MAESTRA —¿Se mantuvieron neutrales los Estados Unidos durante la primera guerra mundial?

EVA —..

MAESTRA —¿Contra qué país declaró guerra el congreso en 1941?

ESTELA —..

MAESTRA —¿En qué año entraron los Estados Unidos en la segunda guerra mundial?

RENE —..

MAESTRA —¿En qué década hubo prosperidad en los Estados Unidos?

CRISTINA —..

MAESTRA —Muy bien. Para mañana estudien la lección que aparece en las páginas 315, 317 y 320 del libro de historia.

SITUATIONAL EXERCISES

You are talking to your students about some important events in the history of the United States. Give them the following information:

1. During the seventeenth century and at the beginning of the eighteenth century, the United States was established.
2. In 1778, George Washington was elected president. Those were the first elections under the Constitution.
3. The Civil War started in 1861. Lincoln was president at that time. He abolished slavery.
4. At the end of the nineteenth century and the beginning of the twentieth century, the United States was already a (world) power.
5. In 1917, the United States entered World War I.
6. In 1929, the Depression started.
7. In 1941, the Japanese bombarded Pearl Harbor, and Congress declared war against Japan.

YOU'RE ON YOUR OWN!

With a classmate, act out the following situation:

Two students are reviewing some important events in the history of the United States before an exam.

VOCABULARY EXPANSION

Some useful words related to history or government:

el, la **alcalde**   mayor
los **aliados**   allies
la **batalla**   battle
el **capitalismo**   capitalism
el **comunismo**   communism
conquistar   to conquer
la **democracia**   democracy
los **esclavos**   slaves
fundar   to found
el, la **gobernador(-a)**   governor
el **gobierno**   government
los **indios**   Indians

la **ley**   law
liberar   to liberate
libre   free
la **monarquía**   monarchy
la **paz**   peace
los **pioneros**   pioneers
los **puritanos**   puritans
los **representantes**   congressmen
los **senadores**   senators
el **territorio**   territory
vencer, derrotar   to defeat

Do you remember the words included in the Vocabulary Expansion?

Complete the following sentences appropriately.

1. Nelson .... a Napoleón en la .... de Waterloo.

2. El comunismo es lo opuesto del ....

3. El sistema de gobierno de los Estados Unidos no es una monarquía; es una

   ....

4. Los .... y los .... forman el congreso y son los que

   hacen las ....

5. Lincoln liberó a los ....

6. Hernán Cortés .... México.

7. En la segunda guerra mundial, los ingleses eran .... de los

   norteamericanos.

8. Terminó la guerra. Ahora tenemos ....

9. Los primeros habitantes de América eran ....

10. No son esclavos. Son hombres ....

11. Antes de ser presidente, Ronald Reagan fue .... de California.

12. Los .... mormones colonizaron Utah, que primero fue un

    .... y después fue un estado.

13. Los españoles .... muchas ciudades en Latinoamérica.

14. Él es el nuevo ………………………… de la ciudad.

15. Los ………………………… vinieron a este país para librarse de la persecución religiosa.

Lesson 13

En la clase de aritmética

Los alumnos acaban de llegar al aula y la maestra empieza la clase de aritmética.

MAESTRA	—¿Quién sabe por qué nuestro sistema de numeración se llama sistema decimal?
CARLOS	—Porque los números aumentan y disminuyen de diez en diez.
MAESTRA	—Muy bien. Aurora, ¿qué son números pares?
AURORA	—Los números que son múltiplos de dos.
RAÚL	—Los números que no tienen mitad son los números impares, ¿verdad?
MAESTRA	—Sí, ¿y qué son números primos?
CARMEN	—Los que sólo son divisibles exactamente por sí mismos o por la unidad.
TERESA	—Los que tienen otros divisores son los números compuestos, ¿no?
MAESTRA	—Sí, Teresa. Diego, ¿sabes cuántas cifras tiene el número 1.[1]042 (mil cuarenta y dos)?
DIEGO	—Tiene cuatro cifras, señorita.
MAESTRA	—Estela, ¿esta cantidad está escrita en números romanos o en números arábigos?
ESTELA	—En números arábigos. Los números romanos se escriben con letras.
MAESTRA	—Bien, ¿qué letras usamos para escribir los números romanos?
CARLOS	—Yo lo sé. Son siete letras; la I que vale uno, la V que vale cinco, la C que vale cien y...
MAESTRA	—Está bien. Sabes la respuesta. Ahora vamos a resolver un problema: El señor Pérez nació en 1913 y murió en 1982. ¿Qué edad tenía cuando murió? Esteban, ¿qué operación tenemos que hacer para resolver el problema?
ESTEBAN	—Tenemos que restar, señorita.
MAESTRA	—Muy bien, pero el 3 es mayor (>) que el 2. ¿Qué tenemos que hacer?
GUADALUPE	—Yo lo sé, señorita. Tenemos que pedirle prestada una decena al 8 y sumarle las 2 unidades.
MAESTRA	—Muy bien; ahora ya podemos quitarle 3 al 12.
ROBERTO	—El señor tenía 69 años cuando murió.
MAESTRA	—Muy bien. A ti te gusta mucho resolver problemas, ¿verdad?
ROBERTO	—Sí, señorita, pero no me gusta estudiar las tablas.
MAESTRA	—Ah, pero es necesario saberlas para poder sacar las cuentas.
EDUARDO	—Señorita, ¿cuándo vamos a estudiar los quebrados?
MAESTRA	—Muy pronto, y después vamos a estudiar los decimales. ¿Hicieron los ejercicios que teníamos para hoy?
MARÍA	—Yo no pude hacerlos porque Ramón me pidió mi libro y no me lo devolvió.
MAESTRA	—Bueno, debes hacerlos para mañana.
RITA	—¿En todos los problemas tenemos que hacer los tres pasos: el planteo, la resolución y la respuesta, señorita?
MAESTRA	—Sí, Rita. Bueno, mañana continuamos. Estudien las medidas lineales.

---

[1]Spanish uses a period instead of a comma between the thousands and the hundreds.

✳ ✳ ✳

In the Arithmetic Class

The students have just arrived (in the classroom) and the teacher starts the arithmetic class.

TEACHER:	Who knows why our numbering system is called the decimal system?
CARLOS:	Because numbers increase and decrease by tens.
TEACHER:	Very good. Aurora, what are even numbers?
AURORA:	The numbers that are multiples of two.
RAUL:	Numbers which don't have halves are odd numbers, right?
TEACHER:	Yes, and what are prime numbers?
CARMEN:	The ones that are only divisible exactly by themselves or by the unit.
TERESA:	The ones that have other divisors are compound numbers, aren't they?
TEACHER:	Yes, Teresa. Diego, do you know how many ciphers the number 1,042 has?
DIEGO:	It has four ciphers, teacher.
TEACHER:	Estela, is this amount written in Roman numerals or Arabic numerals?
ESTELA:	In Arabic numerals. Roman numerals are written with letters.
TEACHER:	Fine, what letters do we use to write Roman numerals?
CARLOS:	I know (it). They are seven letters: the I, which is worth one; the V, which is worth five; the C, which is worth a hundred, and . . .
TEACHER:	Okay. You know the answer. Now we are going to solve a problem: Mr. Perez was born in 1913 and died in 1982. How old was he when he died? Esteban, what operation do we have to do to solve the problem?
ESTEBAN:	We have to subtract, teacher.
TEACHER:	Very good but the 3 is greater (>) than the 2. What do we have to do?
GUADALUPE:	I know (it), teacher. We have to borrow one (a denary) from the 8 and add the two units to it.
TEACHER:	Very good. Now we can take away 3 from 12.
ROBERTO:	The gentleman was sixty nine years old when he died.
TEACHER:	Very good. You really like to solve problems, don't you?
ROBERTO:	Yes, teacher, but I don't like to study the tables.
TEACHER:	Ah, but it is necessary to know them in order to be able to solve arithmetic problems.
EDUARDO:	Teacher, when are we going to study fractions?
TEACHER:	Very soon, and then we're going to study decimals. Did you do the exercises we had for today?
MARIA:	I wasn't able to do them because Ramon borrowed (asked me for) my book and didn't return it to me.
TEACHER:	Well, you must do them for tomorrow.
RITA:	In all problems we have to do the three steps: the operation, the solution, and the answer, teacher?
TEACHER:	Yes, Rita. Okay, we'll continue tomorrow. Study linear measures.

VOCABULARY

COGNATES

arábigo	arabic	**lineal**	linear
la **aritmética**	arithmetic	**múltiplo**	multiple
decimal	decimal	la **operación**	operation
divisible	divisible	**primo**	prime
divisor	divisor	**romano(a)**	Roman
exactamente	exactly		

NOUNS

la **cifra**   cipher
la **decena**   denary
la **medida**   measurement
el **paso**   step
el **planteo**   operation
el **problema**   problem
los **quebrados,** las **fracciones comunes**
   fractions
la **resolución**   solution
el **sistema de numeración**   numbering system
la **unidad**   unit

VERBS

aumentar   to augment, to increase, to go up
devolver (o:ue)   to return, to give back
disminuir   to diminish, to decrease, to go
   down

resolver (o:ue)   to solve
valer[1]   to be worth

ADJECTIVES

compuesto(a)   compound
impar   odd (number)
mayor   bigger, larger
par   even (number)

OTHER WORDS AND EXPRESSIONS

de diez en diez[2]   by tens
pedir prestado(a)   to borrow
por sí mismo   by itself
pronto   soon
sacar cuentas   to work out math problems
   (addition, subtraction, etc.)

LET'S PRACTICE!

Give the Spanish equivalent of the words in parentheses.

1. .... la aritmética.   (*He doesn't like*)

2. Los chicos .... todos los problemas.   (*have just solved*)

3. ¿ .... un número primo?   (*what is*)

4. Ella .... un libro para estudiar las medidas lineales.   (*borrowed*)

5. Nosotros .... los números romanos.   (*have just studied*)

6. .... estudiar las tablas de multiplicar.   (*We don't like*)

7. La maestra .... explicando los quebrados.   (*continued*)

8. Anoche Manuel .... nada porque pasó la noche sacando cuentas.

   (*didn't sleep*)

CONVERSATION

Answer the following questions based on the dialogue.

   1. ¿Por qué nuestro sistema de numeración se llama sistema decimal?

   ....

---

[1]Yo valgo
[2]de + number + en + number = by + number (i.e. contar de dos en dos = to count by twos)

2. ¿Cómo se llaman los números que sólo son divisibles exactamente por sí mismos o por la unidad?

   ....

3. ¿Cómo se llaman los números que son múltiplos de dos?

   ....

4. ¿Qué son números compuestos?

   ....

5. ¿Los números romanos se escriben con números o con letras?

   ....

6. ¿Qué le gusta hacer a Roberto y qué no le gusta hacer?

   ....

7. ¿Para qué dice la maestra que es necesario estudiar las tablas?

   ....

8. ¿Qué van a hacer los chicos muy pronto?

   ....

9. ¿Por qué no pudo María hacer los ejercicios?

   ....

10. ¿Qué tienen que estudiar los niños para mañana?

    ....

Some additional questions:

11. ¿El número 40 es un número par o impar?

    ....

12. ¿El número 19 es un número primo o compuesto?

    ....

13. ¿Cuáles son los divisores del número 24?

    ....

14. ¿Cuántas cifras tiene el número 25.304?

    ....

15. ¿Les enseña Ud. a sus alumnos los números romanos o solamente los números arábigos?

    ....

16. ¿Cuánto vale la letra D en el sistema de numeración romano?

    ....

17. Necesito treinta dólares para comprar un libro y sólo tengo 14. ¿Cuánto me hace falta?

    ....

18. ¿Qué operación tuvo que hacer Ud. para resolver el problema?

    ....

19. ¿Les gusta a sus alumnos resolver problemas?

    ....

20. ¿Qué debemos enseñar primero, los decimales o los quebrados?

    ....

DIALOGUE COMPLETION

Using your imagination and the vocabulary learned in this lesson, complete the missing lines of this dialogue.

Los alumnos de la señora Álvarez se preparan para el examen de aritmética.

MAESTRA —Rafael, ¿cuántas decenas hay en el número 200?

RAFAEL —..

MAESTRA —¿Por qué el número 25 no es par?

CARLOS —..

MAESTRA —¿Qué clase de número es?

TERESA —..

MAESTRA —¿Cómo aumentan y disminuyen los números en nuestro sistema de numeración?

REBECA —..

RAÚL —Señorita, no puedo sacar esta cuenta 72 – 24 porque el cuatro es mayor que el dos.

MAESTRA —..

CARLOS —Señorita, ya es la hora del recreo.

SITUATIONAL EXERCISES

What would you say in the following situations?

1. Ask your students how numbers increase or diminish in the decimal system.
2. Tell a student that she borrowed five books and did not return them.

3. Given the numbers 25 and 19, ask your students which one is bigger.
4. Tell the students what the three steps to solve a problem are.
5. Tell a student who is not very fond of tables that you know that he doesn't like to study the tables, but he has to know them in order to work out many math problems.

YOU'RE ON YOUR OWN!

With a classmate, act out the following situation:

Two students studying for a math exam and quizzing each other

VOCABULARY EXPANSION (Optional)

More words related to Math:

5, 324, 572

unidad de millón
centena de millar
decena de millar
unidad de millar
centena
decena
unidad

$$\begin{array}{r} 3 \\ + 2 \\ \hline 5 \end{array}$$ **sumandos** addend

suma o total total

$$\begin{array}{r} 8 \\ - 4 \\ \hline 4 \end{array}$$ **minuendo** minuend

sustraendo subtrahend

resto o diferencia difference

$$\begin{array}{r} 9 \\ \times 8 \\ \hline 72 \end{array}$$ **multiplicando** multiplicand

multiplicador multiplier

producto product

divisor $$4\overline{)95}$$ $$\begin{array}{r} 23 \\ 8 \\ \hline 15 \\ 12 \\ \hline 3 \end{array}$$

cociente quotient

dividendo dividend

residuo remainder

signos signs

$(+)$ **más**

$(-)$ **menos**

$(\div)$ **entre**

$(\times)$ **por**

Nota In Spanish-speaking countries this division would be in this manner:

dividendo → 95 | 4 ← divisor
15   23 ← (cociente)
(3) ← residuo

Do you remember the words used in the Vocabulary Expansion?

Give the names for the following:

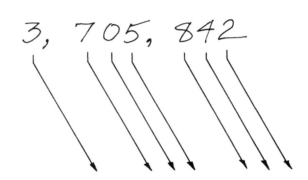

$$
\begin{array}{r}
13 \rightarrow \\
\leftarrow 5\overline{)68} \rightarrow \\
5 \\
\overline{18} \\
15 \\
\overline{(3)} \rightarrow
\end{array}
\qquad
\begin{array}{r}
92 \rightarrow \\
\times\ 3 \rightarrow \\
\overline{276} \rightarrow
\end{array}
\qquad
\begin{array}{r}
24 \rightarrow \\
-18 \rightarrow \\
\overline{6} \rightarrow
\end{array}
\qquad
\begin{array}{r}
72 \rightarrow \\
+\ 24 \rightarrow \\
\overline{96} \rightarrow
\end{array}
$$

$\times$ _____ $\%$ _____ $+$ _____ $-$ _____

3, 705, 842

Lesson 14

Un repaso de aritmética

La señora Paz les había dicho a los alumnos que hoy iba a darles un examen, pero ellos le han pedido un repaso antes del examen.

MAESTRA	—¿Cómo se llaman los términos de las fracciones comunes?
RAFAEL	—Numerador y denominador.
MAESTRA	—¿Qué son números mixtos?
CARMEN	—Los que están formados por un entero y un quebrado.
MAESTRA	—¿Cómo se simplifica un quebrado?
ANA	—Se dividen el numerador y el denominador entre un mismo número.
MAESTRA	—¿Qué hay que hacer para sumar o restar quebrados de distinto denominador?
TERESA	—Se reducen a un común denominador y se suman o restan los numeradores.
MAESTRA	—¿Cuál es el recíproco de ⅘ (cuatro quintos)?
CARLOS	—⁵⁄₄ (cinco cuartos).
MAESTRA	—¿Es ésa una fracción propia o impropia?
EDUARDO	—Es una fracción impropia porque el numerador es mayor que el denominador.
MAESTRA	—Bueno, veo que han estudiado muy bien los quebrados, pero, ¿qué otro tipo de fracciones hay?
RITA	—Las fracciones decimales.
MAESTRA	—¿Qué usamos para separar los enteros de los decimales?
RAÚL	—Usamos el punto[1] decimal.
MAESTRA	—¿Cómo se llama la primera cifra después del punto decimal?
ELVIRA	—Décima.
MAESTRA	—¿Cuál es la equivalencia de ½ (un medio) en decimales?
CARMEN	—Es 0.50 (cincuenta centésimas).
MAESTRA	—¿Y en tanto por ciento?
CARMEN	—Yo lo sé. Es el 50% (cincuenta por ciento).
MAESTRA	—¿Qué por ciento de 8 es 2?
ESTELA	—Es el 25% (veinticinco por ciento).
CARMEN	—Señorita, Ud. nos había dicho que no teníamos que estudiar el tanto por ciento para este examen, ¿verdad?
MAESTRA	—No, el tanto por ciento también va al examen porque ya hace una semana que terminamos esa lección.
MANUEL	—Señorita, ¿cuáles son las medidas de longitud que debemos estudiar?
MAESTRA	—La pulgada, el pie, la yarda y la milla. También deben saber las medidas del sistema métrico decimal.
RICARDO	—¿Todas?
MAESTRA	—No, solamente las medidas de peso.
MARÍA	—¿La libra, la onza y la tonelada?
MAESTRA	—No, el gramo y el kilogramo.

---

[1]In most Spanish-speaking countries, a comma is used instead of a period.

✳ ✳ ✳

A Review of Arithmetic

Mrs. Paz had told her students that today she was going to give them an exam, but they have requested a review before the exam.

TEACHER:	What are the terms of common fractions called?
RAFAEL:	Numerator and denominator.
TEACHER:	What are mixed numbers?
CARMEN:	The ones that are formed by a whole (number) and a fraction.
TEACHER:	How does one reduce a fraction?
ANA:	The numerator and the denominator are divided by the same number.
TEACHER:	What must one do to add or subtract fractions of different denominators?
TERESA:	They are reduced to a common denominator and the numerators are added or subtracted.
TEACHER:	What is the reciprocal of four fifths?
CARLOS:	Five fourths.
TEACHER:	Is that a proper or an improper fraction?
EDUARDO:	It's an improper fraction because the numerator is greater than the denominator.
TEACHER:	Okay, I see that you have studied fractions very well, but what other type of fraction is there?
RITA:	Decimal fractions.
TEACHER:	What do we use to separate the whole (numbers) from the decimals?
RAUL:	We use the decimal point.
TEACHER:	What is the first cipher after the decimal point?
ELVIRA:	Tenth.
TEACHER:	What is the equivalent of ½ (one half) in decimals?
CARMEN:	It's 0.50 (fifty hundredths).
TEACHER:	And in percentage?
CARMEN:	I know. It's 50% (fifty per cent).
TEACHER:	What percentage of eight is two?
ESTELA:	It's 25% (twenty five per cent).
CARMEN:	Teacher, you had told us that we didn't have to study percentage for this exam, right?
TEACHER:	No, percentage is also going to (be included in) the exam because we finished that lesson a week ago.
MANUEL:	Teacher, what are the measurements of length that we must study?
TEACHER:	The inch, the foot, the yard, and the mile. You must also know the measurements of the metric system.
RICARDO:	All of them?
TEACHER:	No, only weight measurements.
MARIA:	The pound, the ounce and the ton?
TEACHER:	No, the gram and the kilogram.

VOCABULARY

COGNATES

el **denominador** denominator	el **numerador** numerator
la **equivalencia** equivalence	el **recíproco** reciprocal
el **gramo** gram	la **yarda** yard
el **kilogramo** kilo, kilogram	

NOUNS

la **centésima** hundredth
la **décima** tenth
el **entero** whole
la **fracción propia, el quebrado propio**
  proper fraction

la **fracción impropia, el quebrado impropio**
  improper fraction
la **libra** pound
las **medidas de longitud (lineales)** lineal
  measures

110

las **medidas de peso** weight measures
la **onza** ounce
el **pie** foot
la **pulgada** inch
el **sistema métrico** metric system
la **tonelada** ton

VERBS

dividir to divide
reducir to reduce
separar to separate
simplificar to simplify

ADJECTIVES

común common

incluído(-a) included
mismo(-a) same
mixto(-a) mixed

OTHER WORDS AND EXPRESSIONS

entre, por by
por ciento per cent
el tanto por ciento percentage
un cuarto one fourth
un medio one half
un quinto one fifth

LET'S PRACTICE!

Rewrite these sentences, putting the italicized verbs first in the *present perfect* and then in the *pluperfect*.

1. Ella *dice* que debemos estudiar las equivalencias.

   ....

   ....

2. *Escriben* todas las medidas de longitud.

   ....

   ....

3. *Hago* la tarea de aritmética.

   ....

   ....

4. *Simplificamos* todas las fracciones.

   ....

   ....

5. ¿Tú les *hablas* del tanto por ciento?

   ....

   ....

6. ¿Ud. lo *divide* por el mismo número?

   ....

CONVERSATION

Answer the following questions based on the dialogue.

1. ¿Qué les habiá dicho la señora Paz a los alumnos?

   ....

2. ¿Qué le han pedido los alumnos a la señora Paz?

   ....

3. ¿Qué son el numerador y el denominador?

   ....

4. ¿Cómo se llaman los números que están formados por un entero y un quebrado?

   ....

5. ¿Cómo se simplifica un quebrado?

   ....

6. ¿Cómo se llama una fracción cuando el numerador es mayor que el denominador?

   ....

7. ¿Qué han estudiado muy bien los alumnos?

   ....

8. ¿Para qué usamos el punto decimal?

   ....

9. ¿Les había dicho la maestra a los niños que no tenían que estudiar el tanto por ciento?

   ....

10. ¿Cuánto tiempo hace que los alumnos terminaron la lección del tanto por ciento?

    ....

11. ¿Qué medidas de longitud tienen que estudiar los niños?

    ....

12. ¿Tienen los niños que estudiar todas las medidas del sistema métrico?

    ....

Some additional questions:

13. ¿Cuántos exámenes les ha dado Ud. a sus alumnos este mes?

    ....

14. ¿Qué clase de número es éste: 5⅜?

   ....

15. ¿Cuál es el común denominador de ½ y ¾?

   ....

16. ¿Cuál es el recíproco de ⅝?

   ....

17. ¿La fracción ⅘ es una fracción propia o una fracción impropia?

   ....

18. ¿Cómo se llama la segunda cifra después del punto decimal?

   ....

19. ¿Cuál es la equivalencia de ⅕ en decimales?

   ....

20. ¿Ya han adoptado (adopted) el sistema métrico en los Estados Unidos?

   ....

21. ¿Cuántas onzas hay en una libra?

   ....

22. ¿Cuántas pulgadas hay en un pie?

   ....

DIALOGUE COMPLETION

Using your imagination and the vocabulary learned in this lesson, complete the missing lines of this dialogue.

Teresa y Ana estudian juntas para el examen de aritmética:

TERESA —Ana, ¿cuáles son las medidas de peso del sistema métrico?

ANA — ....

TERESA —El gramo y el kilogramo sí, pero la libra no.

ANA — ....

TERESA —Hay mil gramos en un kilogramo. ¿Cuántas libras hay en una tonelada?

ANA — ....

TERESA —¿Cuántas décimas hay en dos centésimas?

ANA — ....

TERESA —La yarda y la milla son medidas de longitud.

ANA — ....

TERESA —Usamos el punto decimal para separar los enteros de los decimales.

ANA — ....

TERESA —El número 3½ es un número mixto.

ANA — ....

TERESA —No, no tenemos que estudiar el tanto por ciento para este examen.

SITUATIONAL EXERCISES

What would you say in the following situations?

1. Tell your students the following things about fractions:
   a. To simplify a fraction, the numerator and the denominator are divided by the same number.
   b. To add or subtract fractions of different denominators, they are reduced to a common denominator and the numerators are added or subtracted.
   c. If the numerator is bigger than the denominator, we have an improper fraction.
2. You are reading the following fractions for your students: ⅖; ½; ¾.
3. Tell your students that fractions are going to be included in the exam.

VOCABULARY EXPANSION (Optional)

More words related to Math:

Algunas medidas (Some measurements)

1. **Medidas cuadradas o de superficie** (Square measurements)

   pulgada² (cuadrada)　　**pie² (cuadrado)**　　**acre**
   (square inch)　　　　　　(square foot)　　　　(acre)

2. **Medidas cúbicas o de volumen** (Cubic measurements)

   pulgada³ (cúbica)　　**pie³ (cúbico)**
   (cubic inch)　　　　　(cubic foot)

3. **Medidas de capacidad** (Liquid measurements)

   taza　　**pinta**　　**cuarto**　　**litro**　　**galón**
   (cup)　　(pint)　　(quart)　　(liter)　　(gallon)

4. **Algunas medidas del sistema métrico** (Metric system)

   milímetro　　**centímetro**　　**decímetro**　　**metro**　　**kilómetro**
   (milimeter)　　(centimeter)　　(decimeter)　　(meter)　　(kilometer)

Cifras decimales

$$24.5\ 3\ 8\ 5\ 7$$

cien milésima
diez milésima
milésima
céntesima
décima

Quebrados

$\frac{1}{2}$ (medio) $\frac{2}{3}$ (tercios) $\frac{5}{6}$ (sextos) $\frac{2}{7}$ (séptimos)

$\frac{7}{8}$ (octavos) $\frac{8}{9}$ (novenos) $\frac{6}{10}$ (décimos) $\frac{7}{11}$ (onceavos)

Do you remember the words used in the Vocabulary Expansion?

A. Read the following

1. $23''^2$

2. $12'^3$

3. $\frac{2}{3}$

4. $\frac{3}{7}$

5. $\frac{7}{10}$

6. $\frac{8}{15}$

B. Complete the following sentences.

1. Hay cuatro .... en un galón.

2. La pulgada cuadrada es una medida de .... y el pie cúbico es una

    medida de ....

3. Hay dos .... en un cuarto y hay dos .... en una

    pinta.

4. Un .... tiene mil metros y un metro tiene cien ....

5. Hay 43,560 pies en un ....

6. Un decímetro tiene 100 ....

---

[1]After *tenth* the suffix *-avos* is added to the cardinal number when naming the denominators.

C. Write the names of the following decimal ciphers:

5. 3 8 5 7 2
    ↓ ↓ ↓ ↓ ↓

Lesson 15

En la clase de ciencias

Hacía una semana que las clases habían comenzado y la maestra quería comprobar cuánto recordaban los alumnos sobre ciencias. Hoy va a preguntarles sobre algunos conocimientos básicos.

Astronomía:

MAESTRA —¿Qué es la Tierra?
ÁNGEL —La Tierra es un planeta.
MAESTRA —¿De qué sistema forma parte la Tierra?
RAÚL —Del sistema solar.
MAESTRA —¿Qué es la luna?
CARMEN —Es el satélite de nuestro planeta.
DIEGO —¡A mí me gustaría hacer un viaje a la luna!
MAESTRA —Supongo que algún día todos podremos viajar en el espacio… Sonia, ¿qué es el sol?
SONIA —Es una estrella que nos da energía, luz y calor.
MAESTRA —¿A qué constelación pertenece el sistema solar?
ROSA —A la Vía Láctea.

Física:

MAESTRA —¿Cuáles son los estados en que aparecen los cuerpos en la naturaleza?
RAFAEL —Son tres, maestra: sólido, líquido y gaseoso.
MAESTRA —Raúl, ¿puedes darme un ejemplo de un cuerpo en estado líquido?
RAÚL —El agua, señorita.
MAESTRA —¿Cómo se llama el cambio del estado líquido al estado gaseoso?
CARMEN —Se llama evaporación.
MAESTRA —¿Qué tipos de máquinas simples conocen Uds.?
GUSTAVO —La palanca, la polea, el plano inclinado y el torno.
MAESTRA —Muy bien, Gustavo.

Química:

MAESTRA —¿La sal de cocina es un cuerpo simple o compuesto?
EDUARDO —Es un cuerpo compuesto.
MAESTRA —Pedro, ¿podrías decirme qué elementos componen la sal?
PEDRO —El cloro y el sodio.
MAESTRA —¿Cuál es el nombre científico de la sal de cocina?
CARLOS —Cloruro de sodio.
MAESTRA —¿Cuál es la fórmula del agua?
ESTER —H_2O.
TERESA —¿Qué significa eso?

MAESTRA	—Que en cada molécula de agua hay dos átomos de hidrógeno y un átomo de oxígeno.
RITA	—Señorita, ¿cómo están formados los átomos?
MAESTRA	—¿Quién podría contestarle a Rita?
MARIO	—Yo lo sé. Están formados por protones, electrones, neutrones, etc.
MAESTRA	—Muy bien, Mario. Ya no tenemos más tiempo, pero mañana haremos varios experimentos con la electricidad.

In Science Class

It had been a week since classes started and the teacher wanted to find out how much the students remembered about science.   Today she is going to ask them about some basic knowledge.

Astronomy:

TEACHER:	What is the Earth?
ANGEL:	The Earth is a planet.
TEACHER:	What system is the Earth a part of?
RAUL:	The solar system.
TEACHER:	What is the moon?
CARMEN:	It is our planet's satellite.
DIEGO:	I would like to take a trip to the moon!
TEACHER:	I suppose that some day we will all be able to travel in space . . . Sonia, what is the sun?
SONIA:	It is a star that gives us energy, light and heat.
TEACHER:	To which constellation does the solar system belong?
ROSA:	To the Milky Way.

Physics:

TEACHER:	What are the states in which bodies appear in nature?
RAFAEL:	They are three, teacher: solid, liquid, and gaseous.
TEACHER:	Raul, can you give me an example of a body in a liquid state?
RAUL:	Water, teacher.
TEACHER:	What is the change from the liquid state to the gaseous state called?
CARMEN:	It is called evaporation.
TEACHER:	What types of simple machines do you know?
GUSTAVO:	The lever, the pulley, the inclined plane and the lathe.
TEACHER:	Very good, Gustavo.

Chemistry:

TEACHER:	Is kitchen salt a simple or compound body?
EDUARDO:	It is a compound body.
TEACHER:	Pedro, could you tell me what elements are found in salt?
PEDRO:	Chlorine and sodium.
TEACHER:	What is the scientific name for kitchen salt?
CARLOS:	Sodium chloride.
TEACHER:	What is the formula for water?
ESTER:	H_2O.
TERESA:	What does that mean?
TEACHER:	That in each molecule of water there are two atoms of hydrogen and one atom of oxygen.
RITA:	Teacher, how are atoms formed?
TEACHER:	Who could answer Rita?
MARIO:	I know. They are formed by protons, electrons, neutrons, etc.
TEACHER:	Very good, Mario. We don't have any more time, but tomorrow we will conduct several experiments with electricity.

VOCABULARY

COGNATES

la **astronomía** astronomy	el **hidrógeno** hydrogen
el **átomo** atom	**líquido(-a)** liquid
básico(a) basic	la **molécula** molecule
la **ciencia** science	el **neutrón** neutron
científico(-a) scientific	el **planeta** planet
la **constelación** constellation	el **protón** proton
la **electricidad** electricity	la **sal** salt
el **electrón** electron	el **satélite** satellite
la **energía** energy	**simple** simple
la **evaporación** evaporation	el **sodio** sodium
la **física** physics	**solar** solar
la **fórmula** formula	**sólido(-a)** solid
gaseoso(-a) gaseous	

NOUNS

el **calor**   heat
el **cambio**   change
el **cloro**   chlorine
la **cocina**   kitchen
el **conocimiento**   knowledge
el **ejemplo**   example
el **espacio**   space
la **estrella**   star
la **luna**   moon
la **máquina**   machine
la **naturaleza**   nature
la **palanca**   lever
el **plano inclinado**   inclined plane
la **polea**   pulley

la **Tierra**   Earth
el **tiempo**   time
el **torno**   lathe
la **Vía Láctea**   Milky Way
el **viaje**   trip

VERBS

componer   to compose, to be found in
comprobar (o:ue)   to verify
contestar   to answer
suponer   to suppose

OTHER WORDS AND EXPRESSIONS

cloruro de sodio   sodium chloride
hacer un viaje   to take a trip

LET'S PRACTICE

A.   Rewrite the following sentences, using the future tense.

1. *Vamos a hacer* un experimento con la electricidad.

....

2. *Van a estudiar* la polea y el plano inclinado.

....

3. ¿Dónde *vas a poner* la máquina?

   ....

4. Le *voy a decir* que va a hacer un viaje a la luna.

   ....

B. **Fill in the blanks, using the verbs in the list in the conditional.**

venir   gustar
escribir   saber
salir

1. Él no .... contestar esas preguntas.

2. Yo .... las fórmulas en la pizarra.

3. ¿Tú .... a la conferencia sobre astronomía?

4. A nosotros nos .... viajar en el espacio.

5. Yo .... de mi casa a las ocho.

C. **Write sentences, using the expression *hacía que* and the following elements. Follow the model.**

Modelo: dos años / María / estudiar / ciencias
           Hacía dos años que María estudiaba ciencias

1. 4 horas / ellos / trabajar / cocina

   ....

2. media hora / él / hablarnos / sistema solar

   ....

3. 2 horas / yo / explicarles / eso

   ....

4. 2 días / tú / no comer / nada con sal

   ....

CONVERSATION

Answer the following questions based on the dialogue.

1. ¿Cuánto tiempo hacía que las clases habían comenzado?

   ....

2. ¿Qué quería comprobar la maestra?

   ....

3. ¿Qué es la Tierra?

   ....

4. ¿Cómo se llama el satélite de nuestro planeta?

   ....

5. ¿Qué le gustaría hacer a Diego?

   ....

6. ¿Qué supone la maestra que podremos hacer algún día?

   ....

7. ¿Cuáles son los estados en que aparecen los cuerpos en la naturaleza?

   ....

8. ¿A qué se llama evaporación?

   ....

9. ¿Qué clase de máquinas son el torno y el plano inclinado?

   ....

10. ¿A qué constelación pertenece el sistema solar?

    ....

11. ¿Qué elementos componen la sal?

    ....

12. ¿Qué es el cloruro de sodio?

    ....

13. ¿Cuántos átomos de hidrógeno y de oxígeno hay en cada molécula de agua?

    ....

14. ¿Qué harán los niños mañana?

    ....

Some additional questions:

15. ¿Tienen sus estudiantes algunos conocimientos básicos de física?

    ....

16. ¿Le gustaría a Ud. viajar en el espacio?

    ....

17. ¿El agua es un cuerpo simple o compuesto?

    ....

18. ¿Podría Ud. darme ejemplos de cuerpos sólidos, líquidos y gaseosos?

....

19. ¿Qué significa la formula H_2O?

....

20. ¿Hace Ud. experimentos en la clase?

....

DIALOGUE COMPLETION

Using your imagination and the vocabulary learned in this lesson, complete the missing lines of this dialogue.

Teresa y Anita estudian juntas para el examen de ciencias que tendrán la semana próxima.

TERESA —..

ANITA —Dos. El cloro y el sodio. ¿Cuál es el nombre científico de la sal?

TERESA —..

ANITA —La fórmula del agua es H_2O.

TERESA —..

ANITA —Están formados por protones, electrones y neutrones.

TERESA —..

ANITA —En tres: sólido, líquido y gaseoso. Dame un ejemplo de un cuerpo sólido.

TERESA —..

ANITA —El cambio del estado líquido al estado gaseoso se llama evaporación.

TERESA —..

ANITA —A la Vía Láctea. ¿Por qué es importante el sol?

TERESA —..

ANITA —Bueno, ya no tenemos más tiempo. Mañana continuaremos.

SITUATIONAL EXERCISES

What would you say in the following situations?

You are helping a student with his science lessons. You remind him about the following:

1. *Astronomy:*
   a. The Earth is a planet that is part of the solar system. The Earth's satellite is the moon.
   b. The sun is a star that gives us heat, energy, and light.
   c. The Milky Way is a constellation.

2. *Physics:*
    a. Nature's bodies appear in one of three states: solid, liquid, and gaseous.
    b. The change from the liquid state to the gaseous state is called "evaporation."
    c. There are four types of simple machines: a lever, a pulley, an inclined plane, and a lathe.

3. *Chemistry:*
    a. The scientific name for kitchen salt is sodium chloride.
    b. In each molecule of water, there are two atoms of hydrogen and one atom of oxygen. The formula is H_2O.

YOU'RE ON YOUR OWN!

With a classmate, act out the following situation:

Two students quizzing each other before a science exam

VOCABULARY EXPANSION (Optional)

Other terms related to science:

el **año luz** light year
la **combinación** combination
la **condensación** condensation
disolver (o:ue) to dissolve
filtrar to filter
inorgánico(-a) inorganic
la **materia, sustancia** matter
medir (e:ie) to measure
la **mezcla** mixture

la **onda corta** short wave
la **onda larga** long wave
orgánico(-a) organic
la **pila, batería** battery
las **propiedades** properties
el **símbolo** symbol
la **solidificación** solidification
la **velocidad** speed, velocity

Do you remember the words used in the Vocabulary Expansion?

Complete the following sentences, using the new words.

1. Si disolvemos sal en el agua, tenemos una .... , no una

    ....

2. El .... del oxígeno es O.

3. La .... es el cambio del estado líquido al estado sólido, y la

    .... es el cambio del estado gaseoso al estado líquido.

4. La .... de la luz es 300,000 kilómetros por segundo.

5. Necesito una .... nueva para mi radio.

6. No es una radio de .... corta, es de .... larga.

7. ¿Cuáles son las .... de la materia?

8. Este año estamos estudiando química inorgánica, y el próximo año vamos a estudiar química

    ....

9. El agua tiene tierra.   La tenemos que ………………………… .

10. La distancia de la Tierra a las estrellas se mide en ………………………… .

LESSONS 11–15

VOCABULARY REVIEW

A. Circle the word or phrase that does not belong in each group.

1. pulgada, onza, libra
2. España, Japón, Francía
3. equivalencia, numerador, denominador
4. entero, décima, centésima
5. durar, descubrir, colonizar
6. diez años, década, siglo
7. palanca, tierra, polea
8. estrella, luna, máquina
9. protones, espacio, electrones
10. cloruro de sodio, azúcar, sal
11. resolver, aumentar, disminuir
12. par, mayor, impar
13. divisor, múltiplo, primo
14. única, una sola, todavía
15. arábigo, decena, romano
16. Via Láctea, torno, constelación
17. entero, quinto, medio
18. Holanda, Francia, Japón
19. cuesta, reduce, vale
20. durante, bajo, en esa época
21. además, entonces, en ese caso

B. Circle the word or phrase that best completes each sentence.

1. ¿Qué ocurre cuando el acento (pasa, pronuncia, revisa) de la última sílaba a otra?
2. En la segunda guerra mundial, los Estados Unidos trataron de (librarse, mantenerse, prepararse) neutrales, pero más tarde entraron en la guerra.
3. Japón (comprobó, bombardeó, colonizó) Pearl Harbor.
4. En la palabra *running* (se forma, se castiga, se dobla) la consonante -n delante del sufijo.
5. Se escribe -i antes de -e cuando la combinación está precidida del (acontecimiento, sonido, cambio) *sh*.
6. Olga me pidió prestado el libro y nunca me lo (corrigió, contestó, devolvió).
7. La primera guerra mundial estalló (a principios, a fines, antes) del siglo XX.
8. Tengo un ejemplo, pero eso sólo no (supone, separa, basta).
9. No me gusta la aritmética porque hay que sacar muchas (colonias, cifras, cuentas).
10. A ver… el átomo está formado por electrones, neutrones y (cloro, protones, conocimientos).

11. Aunque Estados Unidos es una gran (constitución, naturaleza, potencia) mundial, también tiene problemas económicos.

12. El congreso declaró la guerra (contra, como, entre) el Japón.

13. Pronto los niños van a poder (cantar, contar, descubrir) de diez en diez.

14. Ayer no (hay, va a haber, hubo) tiempo para enseñarles el tanto por ciento.

15. Diciembre es el (primer, último, cuarto) mes del año.

16. Las colonias estaban (establecidas, incluidas, recibidas) en la costa este.

17. La historia estudia (los acontecimientos, las operaciones, las evaporaciones) más importantes.

18. Los chicos no tienen ningún conocimiento (lineal, mixto, científico).

19. Los números primos sólo son divisibles por (la unidad, un medio, un cuarto) o por sí mismos.

20. En esa (época, naturaleza, palanca) había muchos problemas sociales.

C. **Match the questions in column A with the answers in column B.**

A	B
1. ¿Cuál es el satélite de la tierra? ____	a. Diez.
2. ¿Qué ciencia estudia los planetas? ____	b. En 1929.
3. ¿Qué elementos forman el agua? ____	c. Mixto.
4. ¿Cuántas unidades hay en una decena? ____	d. Sal de cocina.
5. ¿Cuáles son los estados de los cuerpos? ____	e. Planteo, resolución y respuesta.
6. ¿A qué sistema pertenece la tierra? ____	f. Lincoln.
7. ¿Qué otro nombre tiene el cloruro de sodio? ____	g. La astronomía.
8. ¿Cuál es la fórmula del agua? ____	h. En la última.
9. ¿De qué están formadas las moléculas? ____	i. Al sistema solar.
10. ¿Quién era presidente durante la guerra civil? ____	j. No, en el pasado.
11. ¿En qué año empezó la depresión económica? ____	k. H_2O
12. ¿Qué vas a hacer con esos quebrados? ____	l. La luna.
13. ¿Qué clase de número es 3⅘? ____	m. De átomos.
14. ¿Cuáles son los tres pasos para resolver un problema? ____	n. Sólido, líquido y gaseoso.
15. ¿En qué sílaba está el acento en la palabra "nació"? ____	o. Voy a simplificarlos.
16. ¿Está en el presente? ____	p. Hidrógeno y oxígeno.
17. ¿Se escribe la vocal i antes de la e? ____	q. No, sólo las que les di ayer.
18. ¿Es necesario saber todas las reglas? ____	r. El sol.
19. ¿Solamente se puede dividir por sí mismo? ____	s. Generalmente sí, excepto antes de la e.
20. ¿Qué estrella nos da calor y energía? ____	t. Sí, es un número primo.

Name .... Section .... Date ....

D. Crucigrama

HORIZONTAL

3. Va a haber una ____ . Van a elegir un nuevo presidente.
4. Es de Tokío; es ____ .
7. opuesto de *singular*
8. El 4 de julio celebramos el día de la ____ .
10. ⁵⁄₄ es el ____ de ⁴⁄₅.
11. opuesto de *caro*
12. Estudiamos la electricidad en la clase de ____ .
13. Quiero hacer un ____ a México.
15. Vinieron a América buscando principalmente ____ cultivable.
17. Lincoln abolió la ____ .

19. quebrados: ____ comunes
21. La primera ____ mundial comenzó en 1914.
22. Los peregrinos vinieron de ____ .
23. Nuestro sistema de numeración es un sistema ____ .
24. Opuesto de *preguntar*
27. medidas lineales: medidas de ____
29. El kilogramo es una ____ de peso.
32. Vamos a tener un ____ de ortografía.
33. La letra *a* es una ____ .
34. Hay mil gramos en un ____ .
35. No es regular; es ____ .

VERTICAL

1. No es simple; es ____ .
2. personas
5. George Washington fue el primer ____ .
6. Los números pares son ____ por dos.
9. Los ____ vinieron en el "Mayflower" para librarse de la persecución religiosa.
14. Verbo: prosperar; nombre: ____
16. acerca de
18. Hay 3 pies en una ____ .

20. El plano ____ es una máquina simple.
25. opuesto de *multiplicar*
26. Aprendemos cómo se escriben las palabras en la clase de ____ .
28. Hay dos mil libras en una ____ .
30. No es una fracción propia; es una fracción ____ .
31. Verbo: usar; nombre: ____

127

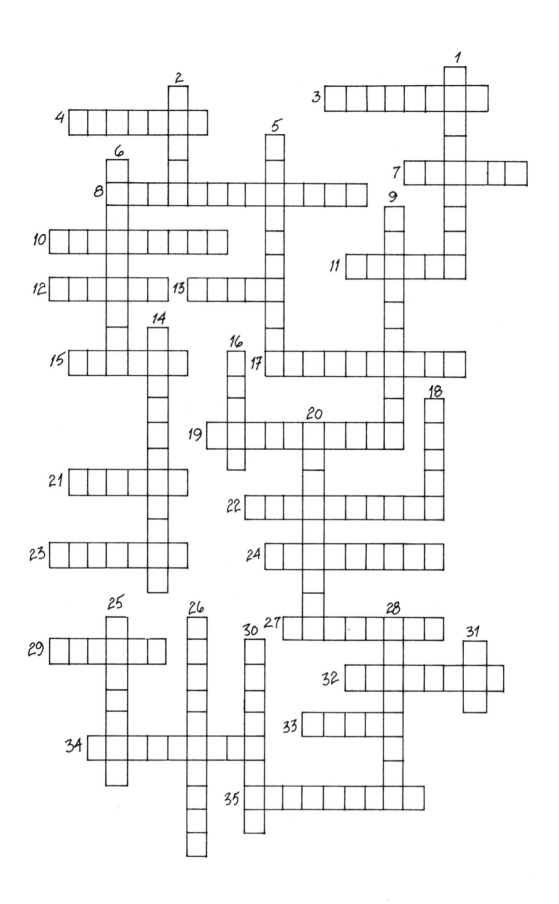

Lesson 16

Con los niños del jardín de infantes

Los niños entran en la clase corriendo y la maestra se enoja un poco.

MAESTRA —¡Niños! ¡Niños! Siempre les digo que no entren corriendo.

SUSANA —¿Nos sentamos en la alfombra, señorita?

MAESTRA —Sí, pero primero quiero que pongan el abrigo en el ropero.

ROSA —Señorita, yo quiero que se siente al lado mío. ¿Nos va a contar un cuento?

MAESTRA —Sí, pero necesito que me ayuden y usen la imaginación.

MIRTA —(*A Carlos, uno de sus compañeros*) ¡Carlos! La señorita quiere que nos sentemos en un círculo...

La maestra les cuenta un cuento, usando unos títeres muy graciosos. Luego saca una caja donde guarda muchas cosas.

MAESTRA —Ahora vamos a ver si ustedes pueden adivinar lo que yo tengo en esta caja.

ANTONIO —¡Yo quiero empezar!

MAESTRA —No, que empiece María. ¡María! Quiero que te pares aquí y que saques una cosa de esta caja.

ALBERTO —¡Dígale que cierre los ojos! ¡Está espiando!

MAESTRA —No, no... Te voy a vendar los ojos, María. Muy bien. (*La niña saca una muñeca.*) Quiero que me digas lo que es.

MARÍA —¡Es una muñeca!

MAESTRA —¡Muy bien, María! (*A los otros niños*) ¡Niños! ¡Están haciendo demasiado ruido! Quiero que estén callados y presten atención.

Los niños sacan muchísimas cosas de la caja: una pelota de tenis, un teléfono, un bloque, una taza para té, etc., etc.

MAESTRA —Ahora vamos a cantar. A ver... Hoy le toca elegir a Dora. Dora, ¿qué quieres que cantemos?

Los niños cantan varias canciones y después arman unos rompecabezas. Cuando suena el timbre para la salida, algunos saltan y corren hacia la puerta.

MAESTRA —¡Niños! Guarden los rompecabezas en el armario. No se olviden de ponerse el abrigo.

ESTELA —Señorita, no encuentro mi chaqueta.

MAESTRA —¿Es ésta? ¿Quieres que te ayude a abrochártela?

ESTELA —Sí... gracias. ¡Hasta mañana, señorita!

Los niños se van y la maestra se queda sola, recogiendo algunas cosas del suelo. Luego apaga la luz y cierra la puerta...

With the Kindergarten Children

The children come into the class running and the teacher gets a little angry.

TEACHER: Children! Children! I'm always telling you not to come in running.
SUSAN: Shall we sit on the rug, teacher?
TEACHER: Yes, but first I want you to put your coats in the closet.
ROSA: Teacher, I want you to sit next to me. Are you going to tell us a story?
TEACHER: Yes, but I need you to help me and use your imagination.
MIRTA: (*To Carlos, one of her classmates*) Carlos! The teacher wants us to sit in a circle . . .

The teacher tells them a story, using some very funny puppets. Then she takes out a box where she keeps many things.

TEACHER: Now we are going to see if you can guess what I have in this box.
ANTONIO: I want to begin!
TEACHER: No, let Maria start. Maria! I want you to stand here and take one thing out of this box.
ALBERTO: Tell her to close her eyes! She's peeking!
TEACHER: No, no . . . I'm going to cover your eyes, Maria. Very good. (*The girl takes out a doll.*) I want you to tell me what it is.
MARIA: It's a doll!
TEACHER: Very good, Maria! (*To the other children*) Children! You're making too much noise! I want you to be quiet and pay attention.

The children take many, many things out of the box: a tennis ball, a phone, a block, a tea cup, etc., etc.

TEACHER: Now we're going to sing. Let's see . . . Today it's Dora's turn to choose. Dora, what do you want us to sing?

The children sing several songs and then put some puzzles together. When the bell rings, some (children) jump and run towards the door.

TEACHER: Children! Put the puzzles away in the cabinet. Don't forget to put on your coats.
ESTELA: Teacher, I can't find my jacket.
TEACHER: Is it this one? Do you want me to help you button it up?
ESTELA: Yes . . . thank you. See you tomorrow, teacher!

The children leave and the teacher is (remains) alone, picking up some things off the floor. Then she turns out the light and closes the door . . .

VOCABULARY

COGNATES

el **bloque** block   el **tenis** tennis

la **imaginación** imagination

NOUNS

la **alfombra** carpet, rug
la **caja** box
la **canción** song
el, la **compañero(-a) de clase** classmate
el **cuento** story, short story
la **chaqueta** jacket
el **jardín de infantes** kindergarten
la **muñeca** doll
el **ojo** eye
la **pelota** ball

el **ropero** closet
el **rompecabezas** puzzle
el **ruido** noise
el **suelo, piso** floor
la **taza** cup
los **títeres** puppets

VERBS

abrochar to fasten, to button
adivinar to guess

130

apagar   to turn off
armar   to put together
cantar   to sing
contar (o:ue)   to tell
correr   to run
espiar   to peek, to spy
enojarse   to get angry
olvidarse (de)   to forget
pararse   to stand
quedarse   to stay, to remain
saltar   to jump

ADJECTIVES

callado(-a)   quiet, silent

demasiado(-a)   too, too much
gracioso(-a), cómico(-a)   funny, comical

OTHER WORDS AND EXPRESSIONS

al lado   beside, next to
al lado mío   next to me
hacia   toward
luego   later
tocarle a uno(-a)   to be one's turn
vendar los ojos   to cover the eyes (i.e. with a
    scarf or handkerchief), to blindfold

LET'S PRACTICE!

Rewrite the following, using the new beginnings and making all the necessary changes.   Follow the model.

Modelo: Los niños arman los rompecabezas.
        Yo quiero que ....
        Yo quiero que los niños armen los rompecabezas.

1. La maestra nos cuenta un cuento.

   Queremos que ....

2. Ellas se sientan en la alfombra.

   La mamá no quiere que ....

3. Yo voy con mis compañeros de clase.

   Ella me sugiere que ....

4. Tú traes las pelotas de tenis.

   Necesitamos que tú ....

5. Nosotros nos enojamos.

   Ellos no quieren que ....

6. Uds. sacan las chaquetas del ropero.

   Les sugiero que ....

7. Tú te olvidas de guardar los títeres en la caja.

   No quiero que ....

8. Los niños se quedan callados.

   La maestra quiere que ....

CONVERSATION

Answer the following questions based on the dialogue.

1. ¿Por qué se enoja un poco la maestra?

   ....

2. ¿Qué les dice siempre la maestra a los niños?

   ....

3. ¿Qué quiere Rosa que haga la maestra?

   ....

4. ¿Cómo quiere la maestra que se sienten los niños?

   ....

5. ¿Qué quiere la maestra que adivinen los alumnos?

   ....

6. ¿Por qué le va a vendar la maestra los ojos a María?

   ....

7. ¿Quiénes están haciendo demasiado ruido?

   ....

8. Además de un bloque y una taza, ¿qué otras cosas sacan los niños de la caja?

   ....

9. ¿A quién le toca elegir hoy lo que van a cantar?

   ....

10. ¿Qué hacen los niños cuando suena el timbre para la hora de salida?

    ....

11. ¿Qué deben guardar los niños en el armario?

    ....

12. ¿Qué hace la maestra cuando se queda sola?

    ....

Some additional questions:

13. ¿Les enseña Ud. a sus alumnos a cantar algunas canciones?

    ....

14. ¿Apaga Ud. siempre todas las luces antes de salir de la clase?

    ....

15. ¿Se enoja Ud. cuando sus alumnos hacen ruido?

    ....

16. ¿Cuántos compañeros tiene Ud. en esta clase?

    ....

17. ¿Le gusta sentarse al lado de la ventana?

    ....

18. ¿Tuvo Ud. alguna vez alumnos del jardín de infantes?

    ....

19. ¿Un maestro necesita tener mucha imaginación?

    ....

DIALOGUE COMPLETION

Using your imagination and the vocabulary you have learned in this lesson, fill in the missing parts of the following dialogue.

La señorita Estévez habla con sus alumnos del jardín de infantes:

ANITA —Señorita, ¿puedo sacar las muñecas del armario?

MAESTRA —..

CARLOS —¿Dónde vamos a sentarnos ahora?

MAESTRA —..

TERESA —¿Puedo sentarme al lado suyo, señorita?

MAESTRA —..

PEPITO —A mí me toca elegir hoy una canción.

MAESTRA —..

PEPITO —La canción que aprendimos ayer.

Después de cantar varias canciones, la maestra les venda los ojos a los niños y ellos tratan de adivinar qué cosas les da.

MAESTRA —¿Qué es esto, Carlos?

CARLOS —..

MAESTRA —Muy bien, Carlos, pero no debes tratar de espiar…

RAÚL —...

MAESTRA —No, hoy no vamos a armar rompecabezas. Marta, ¿dónde está tu chaqueta?

MARTA —...

MAESTRA —Bueno, ya es la hora de salida. Hasta mañana.

SITUATIONAL EXERCISES

What would you say in the following situations?

1. Tell a student that you want him to learn to button up his jacket.
2. Tell your students that you don't want them to sit on the floor.
3. Suggest to a parent that he tell his child not to run in the street.
4. Tell a child that you don't want him to jump in the classroom.
5. Tell a student that you want her to stand next to you and then walk towards the door.
6. Someone wants to choose a song. Tell him/her it's Paco's turn to choose a song.
7. Tell a child that you don't want her to peek, and you're going to cover her eyes.

YOU'RE ON YOUR OWN!

With a classmate, act out the following situation:

Two kindergarten teachers, talking about class activities, materials they use in their classes, problems they have with the children, etc.

VOCABULARY EXPANSION (Optional)

Some articles of clothing:

la **blusa** blouse
la **bufanda** scarf
los **calcetines** socks
la **camisa** shirt
la **camiseta** T-shirt
el **cinto, cinturón** belt
la **falda** skirt
los **guantes** gloves
el **impermeable** raincoat
las **medias** stockings
el **pantalón** pants

¿**cuáles son iguales?** which ones are the same?
el **disco** record
encender (e>ie), prender to turn on
la **película** movie, film
¡**Qué bien cantan!** How nicely you sing!
¿**qué palabra rima con…?** what word rhymes with . . .?
saludar a la bandera to salute the flag
el **televisor** T.V. set
el **tocadiscos** record player

Other useful words and phrases:

¿**cuáles son diferentes?** which ones are different?

Do you remember the words and expressions included in the Vocabulary Expansion?

A. Name the following articles:

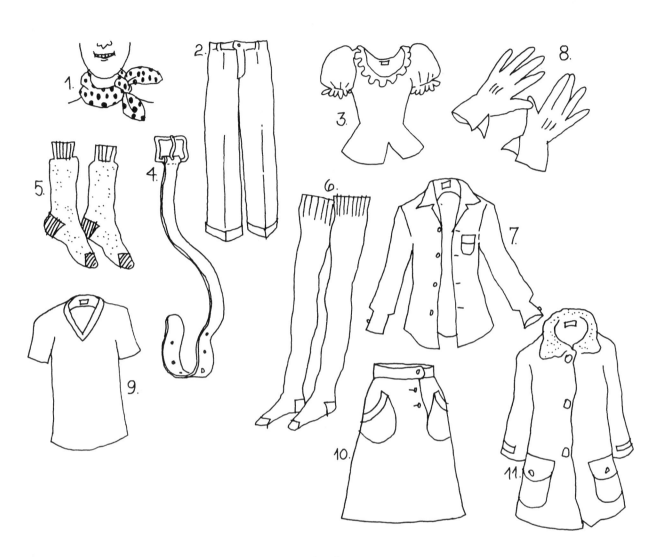

B. Complete the following sentences appropriately.

1. La palabra *canción* .... con *lección*.

2. ¿Por qué apagaron el televisor? Quiero que lo .... otra vez.

3. Ahora vamos a .... a la bandera.

4. Estas palabras son .... , pero estas palabras son diferentes.

5. Fui al cine y vi una .... interesantísima.

6. Uds. ya saben todas las canciones. ¡Y qué bien .... !

7. Tengo muchísimos discos, pero no podemos escucharlos porque aquí no hay

  ....

Lesson 17

Una clase de geometría

Hoy la señora Álvarez va a comenzar el estudio de algunas figuras geométricas, pero antes necesita repasar algunos conceptos básicos.

MAESTRA —Rosa, ¿qué es un ángulo?

ROSA —Es la abertura que forman dos líneas o dos planos que se encuentran en un punto.

MAESTRA —¿Cómo se llama el punto donde se unen las líneas que forman el ángulo?

MARTA —Se llama vértice.

MAESTRA —¿Qué es un ángulo recto?

RAÚL —Es el ángulo formado por dos líneas perpendiculares.

MAESTRA —¿Cuánto mide un ángulo recto?

TERESA —Mide 90 grados.

MAESTRA —¿Qué ángulo forman dos líneas paralelas?

RICARDO —No forman ningún ángulo, señorita. Las paralelas nunca se encuentran.

MAESTRA —Muy bien. Me alegro de que sepas tanto. Pedro, ¿cómo se llama la línea que divide el círculo en dos partes iguales?

PEDRO —Radio, maestra.

TERESA —No, Pedro, es necesario que estudies más. Es el diámetro.

MAESTRA —¿Cómo encontramos el área de un rectángulo?

AURORA —Multiplicando el largo por el ancho.

MAESTRA —¿Y el área de un triángulo?

CARLOS —Multiplicando la base por la altura.

MAESTRA —¿Cómo encontramos el perímetro de un triángulo?

DIEGO —Sumando la longitud de sus lados.

MAESTRA —¿Qué es una circunferencia?

CARMEN —Es el perímetro del círculo.

MAESTRA —Muy bien, Carmen, pero es necesario que esperes a que te pregunte.

RAÚL —Señorita, ¿qué es un segmento?

MAESTRA —Es la parte de una línea comprendida entre dos puntos.

MARÍA —Los segmentos pueden ser rectos o curvos, ¿verdad?

MAESTRA —Muy bien. Raúl, ¿cómo pueden ser las líneas de acuerdo con su posición?

RAÚL —Yo no sé, señorita. Yo no vine a clase la semana pasada.

MAESTRA —Raúl, espero que no faltes más. Es difícil que adelantes si no vienes a clase. ¿Quién sabe la respuesta?

ANA —Yo, señorita. Pueden ser verticales, inclinadas y horizontales.

MAESTRA —Muy bien. Desgraciadamente, no tenemos más tiempo hoy. Continuamos mañana.

A Geometry Class

Today Mrs. Alvarez is going to begin the study of several geometric figures, but first she needs to review some basic concepts.

TEACHER: Rosa, what is an angle?

ROSA: The opening formed by two lines or two planes meeting in a point.

TEACHER: What is the point where the lines that form the angle meet called?

MARTA: It's called the vertex.

TEACHER: What is a right angle?

RAUL: It is the angle formed by two perpendicular lines.

TEACHER: What does a right angle measure?

TERESA: (It measures) ninety degrees.

TEACHER: What angle do two parallel lines form?

RICARDO: They don't form any angle, teacher. Parallels never meet.

TEACHER: Very good. I'm glad you know so much. Pedro, what do they call the line that divides the circle into two equal parts?

PEDRO: Radius, teacher.

TERESA: No, Pedro, you need to study more. It is the diameter.

TEACHER: How do we find the area of a rectangle?

AURORA: By multiplying the length by the width.

TEACHER: And the area of a triangle?

CARLOS: By multiplying the base by the height.

TEACHER: How do we find the perimeter of a triangle?

DIEGO: By adding the length of its sides.

TEACHER: What is a circumference?

CARMEN: It is the perimeter of the circle.

TEACHER: Very good, Carmen, but it is necessary that you wait until I ask you.

RAUL: Teacher, what is a segment?

TEACHER: It is the part of a line between two points.

MARIA: Segments may be straight or curved, right?

TEACHER: Very good. Raul, what can lines be like according to their positions?

RAUL: I don't know, teacher. I didn't come to class last week.

TEACHER: Raul, I hope you don't miss (classes) any more. It is unlikely that you will get ahead if you don't come to class. Who knows the answer?

ANA: I (do), teacher. They may be vertical, inclined and horizontal.

TEACHER: Very good. Unfortunately, we don't have any more time today. We will continue tomorrow.

VOCABULARY

COGNATES

la **base** base	**inclinado(-a)** inclined
la **circunferencia** circumference	**paralelo(-a)** parallel
el **concepto** concept	el **perímetro** perimeter
el **diámetro** diameter	**perpendicular** perpendicular
el **estudio** study	el **plano** plane
la **figura** figure	el **radio** radius
la **geometría** geometry	el **segmento** segment
geométrico(-a) geometric	**vertical** vertical
horizontal horizontal	el **vértice** vertix

NOUNS

la **abertura**   opening
la **altura**   height
el **ancho**   width
el **ángulo**   angle
el **ángulo recto**   right angle
el **grado**   degree
el **lado**   side
el **largo,** la **longitud**   length
el **punto**   point

VERBS

adelantar   to progress
medir (e:i)   to measure

unir   to join

ADJECTIVES

curvo(-a)   curved
recto(-a)   straight

OTHER WORDS AND EXPRESSIONS

de acuerdo con   according to
desgraciadamente   unfortunately
entre   between, among
se encuentran   they meet each other
tanto   so much

LET'S PRACTICE!

Rewrite the following, using the new beginnings.   Follow the model.

Ella adelanta mucho en geometría.
Me alegro de que ....
Me alegro de que ella adelante mucho en geometría.

1. Los alumnos no saben los nombres de las figuras geométricas.

   Es una lástima que ....

2. Repasamos los conceptos básicos.

   Es necesario que ....

3. Mides todos los ángulos.

   No es necesario que ....

4. Entiende la lección de geometría.

   Es difícil que ....

5. Él está entre los alumnos.

   Ojalá que ....

6. ¡Yo estudio tanto!

   ¡Se alegran de que .... !

CONVERSATION

Answer the following questions based on the dialogue.

1. ¿Cómo se llama la abertura de dos líneas que se encuentran en un punto?

   ....

2. ¿Qué es el vértice de un ángulo?

   ....

3. ¿Cómo se llama el ángulo que mide 90 grados?

   ....

4. ¿Qué son líneas paralelas?

   ....

5. ¿De qué se alegra la maestra?

   ....

6. ¿Qué es el diámetro?

   ....

7. ¿Qué es necesario que haga Pedro?

   ....

8. Si en un triángulo multiplicamos la base por la altura, ¿encontramos el área o el perímetro del triángulo?

   ....

9. ¿Cómo se llama el perímetro de un círculo?

   ....

10. ¿Qué es necesario que haga Carmen?

    ....

11. ¿A qué llamamos segmento?

    ....

12. ¿Cómo pueden ser las líneas de acuerdo con su posición?

    ....

13. ¿Qué espera la maestra que haga Raúl?

    ....

Some additional questions:

14. ¿Les enseña Ud. geometría a sus alumnos?

    ....

15. ¿Faltan mucho a clase sus estudiantes?

    ....

16. ¿Cómo se encuentra el área de un cuadrado?

....

17. ¿Cuántos radios hay en un diámetro?

....

18. ¿Cómo se llaman estas dos líneas? ____|____

....

19. ¿Cuántas lados tiene un triángulo?

....

20. ¿Puede nombrar estas líneas de acuerdo con su posición? ___ /

....

DIALOGUE COMPLETION

Using your imagination and the vocabulary learned in this lesson, complete the missing lines of this dialogue.

El señor Roca repasa con sus alumnos algunos conceptos básicos de geometría:

MAESTRO —¿Quién recuerda qué es un ángulo recto?

RITA — ....

MAESTRO —No, Rita, es necesario que estudies más. ¿Ricardo?

RICARDO — ....

MAESTRO —Muy bien. ¿Cómo se llama el punto donde se unen dos líneas que se encuentran? ¿Gonzalo?

GONZALO — ....

MAESTRO —Muy bien. Si sumo la longitud de los lados de un cuadrado, ¿qué encuentro?

RAFAEL — ....

MAESTRO —Y si en un rectángulo multiplico el largo por el ancho, ¿qué encuentro?

MARGARITA — ....

MAESTRO —¿Cómo se llama el perímetro del círculo?

ANA — ....

MAESTRO —La circunferencia, ¿es una línea recta o curva?

ESTELA — ....

MAESTRO —Bien, desgraciadamente tenemos que terminar. Para mañana estudien qué son líneas perpendiculares y líneas paralelas.

SITUATIONAL EXERCISES

What would you say in the following situations?

1. You are telling your students the following things about angles:
   a. An angle is the opening formed by two lines or planes which are joined at one point
   b. The vertex is the point where the two lines meet.
   c. If an angle measures 90 degrees, it is a right angle.
2. You are telling your students how to find the area of some geometric figures:
   a. We find the area of a rectangle (by) multiplying the length by the width.
   b. We find the area of a triangle (by) multiplying the base by the height.
3. One of your students has missed too many classes and is not doing his work. Tell him that you hope he doesn't miss any more classes and that it is necessary that he study. Tell him that, unfortunately, you don't have time to help him after class.

YOU'RE ON YOUR OWN!

With a classmate, act out the following:

Two students quizzing each other before a geometry test

VOCABULARY EXPANSION (Optional)

More words related to Geometry

Ángulos

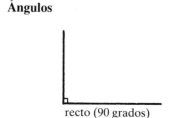 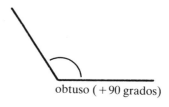 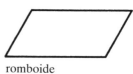

recto (90 grados)   agudo (−90 grados)   obtuso (+90 grados)

Triángulos

 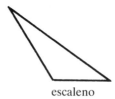

equilátero   isósceles   escaleno

Paralelogramos

cuadrado   rectángulo   rombo   romboide

Otros polígonos

pentágono   hexágono   octógono

Cuerpos

cilindro   esfera   cono   pirámide

142

Name .... Section .... Date ....

Do you remember the words used in the Vocabulary Expansion?

Write the names beside each of the following.

_____   _____   _____   _____

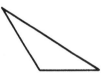

_____   _____   _____   _____

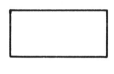

_____   _____   _____   _____   _____

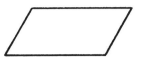

_____   _____   _____   _____

Lesson 18

¡Es la hora del recreo!

La señorita Paz está vigilando a los niños durante el recreo. Camina por el patio de la escuela para ver si hay alguien que la necesite o algún problema que ella tenga que resolver. Ahora está cerca de los columpios.

SRTA. PAZ —¡Juancito! No te pares en el columpio. Siéntate.

ROSITA —¡Ahora me toca a mí! ¡Bájate, Juancito!

SRTA. PAZ —Cuenta hasta veinte y cinco y después deja que otro niño use el columpio.

JUANCITO —¡No hay nadie que quiera usar este columpio! Todos están en las barras...

ROSITA —¡Bájate! ¡Yo quiero usarlo! ¿Por qué no saltas a la cuerda?

JUANCITO —¡Déjame en paz!

SRTA. PAZ —¡Rosita! ¡Cuidado! ¡No te pares delante del columpio!

ADELA —¡Srta. Paz! José me empujó y me caí. ¡Me lastimé!

SRTA. PAZ —¡Ay, no llores! Ve a la oficina ahora mismo y dile a la señora Torres que te ponga una curita.

RAÚL —Srta. Paz, las niñas están tirando arena.

SRTA. PAZ —Diles que voy a mandarlas a la oficina de la directora si siguen haciéndolo.

Vienen dos niñas: una está comiendo dulces y la otra está mascando chicle.

SRTA. PAZ —Teresa, pon ese chicle en el basurero. ¡Carmen! ¡No traigas golosinas a la escuela!

CARMEN —¡Pero señorita Paz! Tengo hambre...

SRTA. PAZ —No creo que tengas hambre cuando acabas de almorzar...

CARMEN —Es que... no almorcé. Mamá me preparó un sándwich de atún y a mí no me gusta el atún...

SRTA. PAZ —Díselo a tu mamá. ¿A dónde vas, Teresa?

TERESA —Al baño.

SRTA. PAZ —No vayas a ése. Es el baño de los maestros.

Ya es hora de volver a la clase. Los estudiantes forman fila delante de sus clases y esperan a sus maestros. Pronto el patio está vacío. "¡Qué paz!", dice la señorita Paz...

✳ ✳ ✳

It's Recess Time!

Miss Paz is watching the children during recess. She walks around the school yard to see if there is anybody who needs her or any problem that she may have to solve. She is now near the swings.

MISS PAZ: Juancito! Don't stand on the swing. Sit down.

ROSITA: Now it's my turn! Get off, Juancito!

MISS PAZ: Count to twenty five and then let another child use the swing.

JUANCITO: There's nobody who wants to use this swing! They're all at the bars . . .

ROSITA: Get off! I want to use it! Why don't you jump rope?

JUANCITO:	Leave me alone!
MISS PAZ:	Rosita! Look out! Don't stand in front of the swing!
ADELA:	Miss Paz! Jose pushed me and I fell. I got hurt!
MISS PAZ:	Oh, don't cry! Go to the office right now and tell Mrs. Torres to put a bandaid on it.
RAUL:	Miss Paz, the girls are throwing sand.
MISS PAZ:	Tell them that I'm going to send them to the principal's office if they continue to do it.

Two girls are coming: one is eating sweets and the other is chewing gum.

MISS PAZ:	Teresa, put that gum in the trash can. Carmen! Don't bring sweets to school!
CARMEN:	But Miss Paz! I'm hungry . . .
MISS PAZ:	I don't believe you're hungry when you have just had lunch . . .
CARMEN:	The fact is . . . I didn't have lunch. Mom made me a tuna sandwich and I don't like tuna . . .
MISS PAZ:	Tell (it to) your mother. Where are you going, Teresa?
TERESA:	To the bathroom.
MISS PAZ:	Don't go to that one. It's the teacher's bathroom.

It is time to go back to class. The students stand in line in front of their classes and wait for their teachers. Soon the yard is empty. "Such peace!", says Miss Paz . . .

VOCABULARY

NOUNS

la **arena**   sand
el **atún**   tuna fish
las **barras**   bars
el **basurero**   trash can
el **columpio**   swing
la **cuerda**   rope
la **curita**   bandaid
el **dulce,** la **golosina**   sweet
la **paz**   peace
el **sándwich**   sandwich

VERBS

contar (o:ue)   to count
dejar   to let, to allow
empujar   to push
lastimar(se)   to hurt, to get hurt

llorar   to cry
preparar   to prepare
tirar   to throw
vigilar   to watch

ADJECTIVE

vacío(-a)   empty

OTHER WORDS AND EXPRESSIONS

ahora mismo   right now
¡cuidado!   look out!, be careful!
déjame en paz   leave me alone
delante de   in front of
formar fila   to line up
saltar a la cuerda   to jump rope

LET'S PRACTICE

A.   **Rewrite the following, using the new beginnings.   Make all necessary changes.**

Modelo: Estoy segura de que puede venir.
No estoy segura ....
No estoy segura de que pueda venir.

1. Aquí hay muchos niños que saben saltar a la cuerda.

   ¿Hay alguien aquí que .... ?

2. Hay dos niños que quieren usar los columpios vacíos.

   No hay nadie que ....

3. Busco un lugar donde vendan sándwiches.

   Conozco ....

4. Estoy segura de que podemos resolver los problemas.

   Dudo ....

5. Creo que están tirando arena.

   No creo ....

B. **Complete the following sentences, using the Spanish equivalent of the words in parentheses. Use the *tú* form.**

1. ¡Rosita! ¡ .... ! (*Don't cry!*)

2. ¿El chicle? .... en el basurero. (*Put it*)

3. ¿El sándwich de atún? .... (*Give it to her.*)

4. ¡Cuidado! ¡ .... ! (*Don't get hurt!*)

5. ¡Mario! ¡ .... de las barras! (*Get off*)

6. ¡Juancito! ¡ .... a la oficina de la directora! (*go*)

7. ¿La tarea? ¡ .... ahora mismo! (*Do it*)

8. .... que venga. (*Tell her*)

9. ¡Robertito! ¡ .... eso! (*Don't do*)

10. No, Anita. ¡ .... al patio ahora! (*Don't go out!*)

11. Raúl, ¡ .... aquí ahora mismo! (*come!*)

12. ¿El dinero? .... (*Don't give it to him!*)

13. ¡Graciela! ¡ .... delante de los columpios! (*Don't stand!*)

14. ¡ .... ! (*Leave me alone!*)

15. ¡Jorge! ¡ .... ! (*Don't push her.*)

CONVERSATION

Answer the following questions based on the dialogue.

1. ¿Qué está haciendo la señorita Paz durante el recreo?

   ....

2. ¿Para qué camina por el patio de la escuela?

....

3. ¿Qué le dice a Juancito?

....

4. ¿Qué le dice Rosita a Juancito?

....

5. ¿Hasta qué número tiene que contar Juancito?

....

6. ¿Por qué dice Juancito que puede quedarse en el columpio?

....

7. ¿Qué le sugiere Rosita a Juancito?

....

8. ¿Qué no quiere la señorita Paz que haga Rosita?

....

9. ¿Cómo se cayó Adela?

....

10. ¿Qué están haciendo las niñas con la arena?

....

11. ¿Dónde tiene que poner Teresa el chicle?

....

12. ¿De qué era el sándwich que preparó la mamá de Carmen?

....

13. ¿Dónde forman fila los niños después del recreo?

....

14. ¿Por qué dice "¡qué paz!" la maestra?

....

Some additional questions:

15. ¿Vigila Ud. a los niños durante el recreo?

....

16. ¿Hay algún problema que Ud. necesite resolver?

    ....

17. ¿Tienen Uds. barras y columpios en su escuela?

    ....

18. ¿Ud. les deja comer golosinas a los niños?

    ....

19. ¿Le gusta a Ud. el atún?

    ....

20. ¿Sus alumnos forman fila antes de entrar en la clase?

    ....

DIALOGUE COMPLETION

Use your imagination and the vocabulary you have learned in this lesson to fill in the missing parts of the following dialogue.

En el patio de la escuela, durante el recreo:

MAESTRA   —¡Elenita! ¡Bájate del columpio!

ELENITA   —...

MAESTRA   —Porque ahora le toca a Teresa.

ELENITA   —...

TERESA   —No, yo no quiero saltar a la cuerda. Yo quiero usar el columpio.

MAESTRA   —¡Carmen! ¿Por qué lloras?

CARMEN   —...

MAESTRA   —No llores. Ven acá para ponerte una curita. Jorge, ¿por qué empujaste a Carmen?

JORGE   —...

MAESTRA   —Eso no es verdad. Fuiste tú, no Carlos.

ROSA   —Señorita, tengo hambre. ¿Puedo ir a comprar un dulce?

MAESTRA   —...

ROSA   —Pero señorita... A mí me gustan los dulces...

MAESTRA —Sí, Rafael.   Ya sonó el timbre.   Deben formar fila.

SITUATIONAL EXERCISES

You have yard duty at your school.   This is the situation you find.   Tell each child what to do (or not to do).

1. Pedro is chewing gum and Olga is eating sweets.
2. Roberto is pushing a girl.
3. Juancito is standing on the swing.
4. Paco won't get off the swing and it is Maria's turn.
5. Raquel is standing in front of a swing.
6. Carlos is throwing sand.
7. Jorge cut himself and needs a bandaid.
8. Beto is walking towards the teachers' bathrooms.
9. Marta's hands are dirty.
10. Teresa isn't eating her lunch.

YOU'RE ON YOUR OWN!

With a classmate, act out the following situation:

Two teachers who are sharing yard duty, commenting on all the activities and problems they encounter during recess and lunch time.

VOCABULARY EXPANSION (Optional)

Some children's favorites:

el **batido**   milkshake
la **galletita**   cookie
la **hamburguesa**   hamburger
las **papas fritas**   French fries

las **papitas fritas**   potato chips
el **pastel**   pie
el **perro caliente**   hot dog
la **torta**   cake

helado de
ice-cream
{ **chocolate**
fresas   strawberry
vainilla

jugo de
juice
{ **naranje**   orange
tomate
toronja   grapefruit
manzana   apple
uvas   grapes
piña   pineapple

sándwich de
{ **jamón y queso**   ham and cheese
ensalada de huevo   egg salad
pollo   chicken
mantequilla de maní y jalea   peanut butter and jelly

Do you remember the words used in the Vocabulary Expansion?

Help your American students to order the following at a fast-food restaurant in a Latin American country:

John wants: a hamburger   ....

                       French fries   ....

                       tomato juice   ....

                       apple pie   ....

Bill wants: a hot dog   ....

                       potato chips   ....

                       orange juice   ....

                       chocolate ice cream   ....

Michelle wants: a chicken salad sandwich   ....

                       grape juice   ....

                       strawberry cake   ....

Wendy wants: a ham and cheese sandwich   ....

                       grapefruit juice   ....

                       vanilla milkshake   ....

Jim wants: a peanut butter and jelly   ....

                          sandwich   ....

                       pineapple juice   ....

                       cookies   ....

Sandra wants: egg salad sandwich   ....

                       apple juice

151

Lesson 19

Una clase de higiene

El señor Chávez, maestro de cuarto grado, está en el salón de clase. En cuanto los niños vuelvan del recreo, les va a hablar de algo muy importante: la salud. ¡Ah! Aquí llegan los niños y se sientan, listos para escuchar al maestro.

MAESTRO	—Espero que hayan leído el capítulo diez, como les dije ayer. ¿De qué se trata ese capítulo?
OSCAR	—De la nutrición y los buenos hábitos de limpieza.
MAESTRO	—¡Muy bien, Oscar! Una dieta balanceada es esencial para la buena salud. ¿Por qué es eso? ¿Silvia?
SILVIA	—Porque necesitamos comer diferentes clases de alimentos para que nuestro cuerpo tenga las vitaminas que necesita.
MAESTRO	—Sí, es verdad... pero ¿qué otros elementos nutritivos necesita el cuerpo?
ANA	—Proteína, minerales y... y...
MAESTRO	—... Y carbohidratos. ¡Muy bien, Ana! ¿Para qué necesitamos proteína?
ESTER	—Para el crecimiento, la reparación y el mantenimiento de los tejidos.
MAESTRO	—¡Excelente, Ester! ¿Y los carbohidratos?
HUGO	—Los carbohidratos dan energía. Tan pronto como llegue a casa voy a comer un pedazo de pastel, porque estoy muy débil.
MAESTRO	—(*Se ríe con los niños*) Bueno, un pedazo de pastel de vez en cuando está bien. —Pero... ¿qué pasa cuando se consumen demasiados carbohidratos?
TERESA	—El cuerpo retiene lo que no se necesita y se convierte en grasa.
ALBERTO	—Y entonces la persona engorda...
MAESTRO	—¡Exactamente! El cuerpo no necesita mucha grasa, en realidad... unas dos o tres onzas por día... ¿Qué minerales son importantes para la salud?
FEBE	—El hierro, el calcio y el fósforo.
MAESTRO	—Muy bien. Hay catorce minerales que son esenciales para una buena dieta.
CARLOS	—También es importante comer despacio y masticar bien las comidas.
MAESTRO	—Me alegro de que te hayas acordado de eso, Carlos. Es muy importante. ¿Qué otras cosas son importantes?
RAÚL	—Practicar deportes... hacer ejercicios...
NORA	—También necesitamos aire puro. Un cuarto debe tener buena ventilación.
ESTELA	—La limpieza es muy importante...
MAESTRO	—¡Muy bien! La higiene personal es importantísima. ¿Qué hay que hacer todos los días?
MARÍA	—¡Bañarse! Y cepillarse los dientes tres veces al día, y lavarse las manos antes de comer.
ANA	—Mamá no nos permite sentarnos a la mesa a menos que nos lavemos las manos...
MAESTRO	—¡Muy bien! Mañana vamos a hablar de algunas enfermedades y de cómo prevenirlas. Ya saben el dicho: "Es mejor prevenir que curar."

A Hygiene Class

Mr. Chavez, the fourth grade teacher, is in the classroom. As soon as the children come back from recess, he's going to talk to them about something very important: health. Ah! The children arrive and sit down, ready to listen to the teacher.

TEACHER:	I hope you have read chapter ten, as I told you yesterday. What is that chapter about?
OSCAR:	About nutrition and good habits of cleanliness.
TEACHER:	Very good, Oscar! A balanced diet is essential for good health. Why is that? Silvia?
SILVIA:	Because we need to eat different kinds of food so that our bodies will have the vitamins it needs.
TEACHER:	Yes, it is true . . . but what other nutritional elements does the body need?
ANA:	Protein, minerals and . . . and . . .
TEACHER:	. . . And carbohydrates. Very good, Ana! What do we need protein for?
ESTER:	For the growth, repair and maintenance of tissue.
TEACHER:	Excellent, Esther! And carbohydrates?
HUGO:	Carbohydrates supply energy. As soon as I get home, I'm going to eat a piece of pie, because I'm very weak.
TEACHER:	(*Laughing with the children*) Well, a piece of pie once in a while is okay. But . . . What happens when one consumes too many carbohydrates?
TERESA:	The body retains what it doesn't need and it turns into fat.
ALBERTO:	And then the person gets fat . . .
TEACHER:	Exactly! The body doesn't need much fat, really. . . about two or three ounces a day . . . What minerals are important for (good) health?
FEBE:	Iron, calcium and phosphorus.
TEACHER:	Very good. There are fourteen minerals that are essential to a good diet.
CARLOS:	It is also important to eat slowly and chew the food well.
TEACHER:	I'm glad you have remembered that, Carlos. It is very important. What other things are important?
RAUL:	To play sports . . . to exercise . . .
NORA:	We also need fresh air. A room should have good ventilation.
ESTELA:	Cleanliness is very important . . .
TEACHER:	Very good! Personal hygiene is extremely important. What must one do every day?
MARIA:	Bathe! And brush one's teeth three times a day, and wash one's hands before eating.
ANA:	Mom doesn't allow us to sit at the table unless we wash our hands . . .
TEACHER:	Very good! Tomorrow we are going to talk about some diseases and about how to prevent them. You know the saying: An ounce of prevention is worth a pound of cure.

VOCABULARY

COGNATES

balanceado(-a) balanced	la **higiene** hygiene
el **calcio** calcium	el **mineral** mineral
el **carbohidrato** carbohydrate	la **nutrición** nutrition
la **dieta** diet	**personal** personal
esencial essential	la **proteína** protein
excelente excellent	la **ventilación** ventilation
el **fósforo** phosphorus	la **vitamina** vitamin
el **hábito** habit	

NOUNS

el **capítulo** chapter
el **crecimiento** growth
el **cuarto** room
el **deporte** sport
el **dicho** saying
el **diente** tooth
la **enfermedad** sickness, disease
la **grasa** fat
el **hierro** iron
la **limpieza** cleanliness
el **mantenimiento** maintenance
el **pastel** pie
el **pedazo, trozo** piece
la **reparación** repair
la **salud** health
los **tejidos** tissue

VERBS

cepillar(se) to brush
consumir to consume

convertirse (e:ie) (en) to turn into
curar to cure
engordar to get fat
prevenir (*conj. like* **venir**) to prevent
prevenir (conj. like *venir*) to prevent
reír(se)[1] to laugh
retener (*conj. like* **tener**) to retain

ADJECTIVES

débil weak
nutritivo(-a) nourishing

OTHER WORDS AND EXPRESSIONS

el **aire puro** fresh air
al día a day, per day
despacio slowly
en realidad in fact
hacer ejercicios to exercise
practicar deportes to take part in sports

LET'S PRACTICE

Complete the following, using the Spanish equivalent of the words in parentheses.

1. No creo que él .... todas

   esas enfermedades. (*has had*)

2. Vamos a tener la clase de higiene ....

   .... (*as soon as they return*).

3. Necesitas una dieta balanceada ....

   .... todas las vitaminas que necesita.

   (*so that your body has*)

4. Siempre me cepillo los dientes ....

   de almorzar. (*when I finish*)

5. No puedes sentarte a la mesa ....

   .... (*unless you wash your hands*).

---

[1](me) río, (te) ríes, (se) ríe, (nos) reímos, (se) ríen

155

6. No creo que ellos ya ....

   el capítulo sobre la nutrición.   (*have studied*)

7. Voy a tratar de salir sin que los chicos ....

   (*see me*)

8. No me permitió salir ....

   la limpieza de la casa.   (*until I finished*)

CONVERSATION

Answer the following questions based on the dialogue.

1. ¿De qué les va a hablar el señor Chávez a los niños en cuanto vuelvan del recreo?

   ....

2. ¿Qué espera el señor Chávez que hayan hecho los niños?

   ....

3. ¿De qué trata el capítulo diez?

   ....

4. ¿Qué es esencial para la buena salud?

   ....

5. ¿Qué elementos nutritivos necesita el cuerpo?

   ....

6. ¿Qué necesitamos para el mantenimiento, la reparación y el crecimiento de los tejidos?

   ....

7. ¿Qué dan los carbohidratos?

   ....

8. ¿Qué va a hacer Hugo en cuanto llegue a su casa?

   ....

9. ¿Qué pasa cuando se consumen demasiados carbohidratos?

   ....

10. ¿Qué son el hierro, el fósforo y el calcio?

....

11. ¿Por qué hay que bañarse todos los días?

....

12. ¿De qué van a hablar mañana?

....

Some additional questions:

13. ¿Qué va a hacer Ud. en cuanto llegue a su casa?

....

14. ¿Les habla Ud. a sus alumnos de los buenos hábitos de limpieza?

....

15. ¿Tiene Ud. una dieta balanceada?

....

16. ¿Qué hace Ud. cuando se siente débil?

....

17. ¿Qué comidas cree Ud. que engordan mucho?

....

18. ¿Come Ud. un pedazo de pastel de vez en cuando?

....

19. ¿Tiene buena ventilación el aula de Uds.?

....

20. ¿Qué hábitos de higiene personal cree Ud. que son importantes?

....

21. ¿Practica Ud. deportes?

....

22. ¿Se ríe Ud. con sus alumnos a veces?

....

DIALOGUE COMPLETION

Using your imagination and the vocabulary learned in this lesson, complete the missing lines of this dialogue.

Los niños han terminado de estudiar el capítulo que trata sobre la salud, y la maestra les hace algunas preguntas para ver si lo han comprendido.

MAESTRA	—¿Cuántas veces al día debemos cepillarnos los dientes?
INÉS	—..
MAESTRA	—¿Qué cantidad de grasa necesita nuestro cuerpo cada día?
RITA	—..
MAESTRA	—¿En qué se convierten los carbohidratos que nuestro cuerpo no necesita?
FLORA	—..
MAESTRA	—Tomás, ¿para qué necesitamos las proteínas?
TOMÁS	—..
MAESTRA	—Excelente, Tomás. Carlos, ¿qué alimentos dan energía?
CARLOS	—..
MAESTRA	—Muy bien.
FERNANDO	—..
MAESTRA	—El hierro, el calcio y el fósforo. Paco, ¿qué otros hábitos de higiene son importantes?
PACO	—..
MAESTRA	—Muy bien. Mañana continuamos.

SITUATIONAL EXERCISE

What would you say in the following situation?

You are talking to your students about health.   You tell them the following:

1. A balanced diet is essential for good health because we need to eat different kinds of food so that our bodies have all the vitamins, protein, minerals, and carbohydrates they need.

2. When one consumes too many carbohydrates, the body retains what it does not need, and turns it into fat. The body does not need much fat, really; only about two or three ounces a day.

3. Other things that are important are: fresh air and personal hygiene, also to exercise and take part in sports.

4. It is very important to bathe every day, brush one's teeth three times a day, and wash one's hands before eating.

5. Remember the saying: an ounce of prevention is better than a pound of cure.

YOU'RE ON YOUR OWN!

With a classmate, act out the following situation:

A teacher and a student discussing nutrition and personal hygiene

VOCABULARY EXPANSION (Optional)

Algunos deportes

el **básquetbol, baloncesto**   basketball
el **béisbol**   baseball
el **fútbol**   soccer
el **fútbol americano**   football

la **gimnasia**   gymnastics
la **natación**   swimming
el **tenis**   tennis
el **vólibol**   volleyball

Algunas enfermedades

la **difteria**   diphtheria
las **paperas**   mumps
la **poliomielitis**   poliomyelitis
la **rubeola**   German measles, rubella

el **sarampión**   measles
el **tétano**   tetanus
la **tos ferina**   whooping cough
la **varicela**   chickenpox

Otras palabras útiles (Other useful words)

alérgico(-a)   allergic
contagioso(-a)   contagious
estar vacunado(-a) contra   to be vaccinated
   against
la **medicina**   medicine

Complete the following sentences, using the Spanish equivalent of the words in parentheses:

1. No jugamos .... ; jugamos ....

   (*soccer / football*)

2. La .... y la .... son enfermedades muy

   .... (*whooping cough / chickenpox / contagious*)

3. Mis hijos .... el .... , la .... y la

   .... (*are vaccinated against / tetanus / poliomyelitis / diphtheria*)

4. No podemos jugar .... ni .... porque no tenemos las

   pelotas.   (*basketball / volleyball*)

5. ¿Es Ud. .... a alguna .... ?   (*allergic / medicine*)

6. Mis .... favoritos son la .... y el ....

   (*sports / swimming / baseball*)

7. Cuando yo era niña tuve .... y .... (*mumps /
   German measles*)

8. Me gusta mucho la .... (*gymnastics*)

Lesson 20

¡Trabajemos juntos!

La señorita García está hablando con un grupo de padres sobre algunas de las reglas de la escuela, y pidiéndoles su cooperación para que, juntos padres y maestros, puedan hacer que los niños se beneficien y aprovechen bien el año escolar.

SRTA. GARCÍA —Un problema que tenemos es que algunos niños llegan a la escuela demasiado temprano. Si están aquí una hora antes de que empiecen las clases, no tienen supervisión.

SRA. VARGAS —Yo tengo que ir a trabajar, y no quiero dejar a mi hija sola en casa.

SRTA. GARCÍA —Comprendo, pero sería mejor si su hija pudiera quedarse en la casa de alguna amiga o vecina hasta la hora de venir a la escuela.

SR. TORRES —Señorita García, mi hijo trajo su bicicleta el mes pasado y se la robaron…

SRTA. GARCÍA —Si los niños vienen en bicicleta, tienen que tener un candado y ponerlas en el lugar donde se guardan las bicicletas.

SRA. GÓMEZ —Mi hijo viene en el ómnibus escolar, y el otro día perdió el ómnibus y tuvo que quedarse en casa.

SRTA. GARCÍA —¡Qué lástima! Eso no pasaría si el niño estuviera en la parada de ómnibus unos diez minutos antes de la llegada del autobús.

SR. SOTO —El otro día mi hija llegó tarde porque tuvo que ir al dentista y la maestra la dejó sin recreo.

SRTA. GARCÍA —Si un niño tiene cita con el médico o con el dentista, hagan el favor de darle una notita para el maestro.

SRA. VARGAS —¿Y si los chicos estuvieran enfermos pero no fueran al médico?

SRTA. GARCÍA —Nosotros les dijimos a los niños que siempre trajeran una nota de los padres al volver a la escuela, explicando la razón de la ausencia.

SR. TORRES —Bueno, cambiando de tema… yo creo que el almuerzo de la cafetería es muy caro. Yo tengo tres hijos en la escuela, y es mucho dinero para mí.

SRTA. GARCÍA —Ud. puede solicitar un almuerzo más barato o gratis, según el sueldo que reciba… Yo puedo darle una planilla para llenar.

SRA. GÓMEZ —Mi hijo muchas veces pierde el dinero que le doy para el almuerzo.

SRTA. GARCÍA —Sería mejor si pusiera el dinero en un sobre cerrado antes de dárselo al niño.

SR. SOTO —Tenemos una sobrina que está de visita en casa. ¿Puede venir a la escuela con mi hija?

SRTA. GARCÍA —Lo siento, señor Soto, pero si permitiéramos visitas de niños que no están matriculados en la escuela, los maestros tendrían mucho más trabajo.

La Srta. García les agradece a los padres que hayan venido y les pide que, si es posible, trabajen como voluntarios para ayudar a los niños de la escuela.

✱ ✱ ✱

Let's Work Together!

Miss Garcia is speaking with a group of parents about some of the school regulations, and asking them for their cooperation so that, together as parents and teachers, they can make sure that the children will benefit by and make good use of the school year.

MISS GARCIA:	One problem we have is that some children arrive at school too early. If they are here one hour before classes start, they don't have (any) supervision.
MRS. VARGAS:	I have to go to work, and I don't want to leave my daughter alone in the house.
MISS GARCIA:	I understand, but it would be better if your daughter could stay at some friend's or neighbor's house until it's time to come to school.
MR. TORRES:	Miss Garcia, my son brought his bicycle last month and it was stolen . . .
MISS GARCIA:	If the children ride their bicycles, they have to have a padlock and put them on the bicycle rack.
MRS. GOMEZ:	My son rides the school bus, and the other day he missed the bus and had to stay home.
MISS GARCIA:	What a pity! That wouldn't happen if the child were at the bus stop about ten minutes before the bus gets there.
MR. SOTO:	The other day my daughter was late because she had to go to the dentist and the teacher didn't let her have recess.
MISS GARCIA:	If a child has an appointment with the doctor or with the dentist, please give him a note for the teacher.
MRS. VARGAS:	And if the children were sick but didn't go to the doctor?
MISS GARCIA:	We told the children to always bring a note from the parents upon returning to school, explaining the reason for the absence.
MR. TORRES:	Well, not to change the subject, but . . . I think the cafeteria lunch is very expensive. I have three children in school, and it is a lot of money for me.
MISS GARCIA:	You can apply for a cheaper or free lunch, according to the salary you receive . . . I can give you a form to fill out.
MRS. GOMEZ:	My son often loses the money that I give him for lunch.
MISS GARCIA:	It would be better if you put the money in a sealed envelope before giving it to the child.
MR. SOTO:	We have a niece who is visiting at home. May she come to school with my daughter?
MISS GARCIA:	I'm sorry, Mr. Soto, but if we were to allow visits from children who are not enrolled in the school, the teachers would have much more work.

Miss Garcia thanks the parents for having come and asks that, if possible, they work as volunteers to help the children at school.

VOCABULARY

COGNATES

la **cooperación**	cooperation	la **supervisión**	supervision
la **nota**	note	el, la **voluntario(-a)**	volunteer

NOUNS

el **almuerzo**	lunch	la **planilla, forma**	form
la **ausencia**	absence	la **razón**	reason
el **candado**	padlock	el **sobre**	envelope
la **cita**	appointment	el **sueldo**	salary
la **llegada**	arrival	el **tema**	subject, topic

162

VERBS

agradecer[1]   to thank
aprovechar   to make good use of, to take
  advantage of
beneficiarse de   to benefit
comprender   to understand
llenar   to fill out
matricularse   to enroll, to register
perder (e:ie)   to miss (i.e. the bus)
robar   to steal
solicitar   to apply

ADJECTIVES

caro(a)   expensive

cerrado(a)   sealed
escolar   school
gratis   free
matriculado(a)   enrolled, registered

OTHER WORDS AND EXPRESSIONS

de visita   visiting
en casa   at home
haga(n) (haz) el favor de   please
parada de ómnibus   bus stop
¡Qué lástima!   that's too bad, what a pity
según   according to

LET'S PRACTICE!

Rewrite the following, using the new beginnings and making all necessary changes.

1. Quiere que yo traiga un candado.

   Quería ....

2. No creo que él sepa llenar la planilla.

   No creía ....

3. No es verdad que estén de visita en casa.

   No era verdad ....

4. Esperamos que se matriculen esta semana.

   Esperábamos ....

5. Quieren que esperemos la llegada del avión.

   Querían ....

6. Te sugiero que sirvas el almuerzo temprano.

   Te sugerí ....

7. No hay nadie que me comprenda.

   No había nadie ....

8. Busco una casa que no sea cara.

   Buscaba ....

----

[1]yo agradezco

9. Iré a verte si tengo tiempo.

   Iría ....

10. Lo haremos si podemos.

    Lo haríamos ....

CONVERSATION

Answer the following questions based on the dialogue.

1. ¿Sobre qué está hablando la señorita García?

   ....

2. ¿Qué les está pidiendo a los padres?

   ....

3. ¿Qué pasa si los niños llegan a la escuela una hora antes de que empiecen las clases?

   ....

4. ¿Dónde seriá mejor que se quedara la hija de la Sra. Vargas?

   ....

5. ¿A quién le robaron la bicicleta el mes pasado?

   ....

6. ¿Qué deben tener los niños que vienen a la escuela en bicicleta?

   ....

7. El otro día, el hijo de la señora Gómez tuvo que quedarse en casa. ¿Por qué?

   ....

8. ¿Cuánto tiempo antes de la llegada del ómnibus deben estar los niños en la parada?

   ....

9. ¿Por qué llegó tarde a clase la hija del señor Soto?

   ....

10. ¿Cuándo deben traer los niños una nota de sus padres?

    ....

11. ¿Qué dice el señor Torres sobre el almuerzo en la cafetería?

    ....

12. ¿Qué puede solicitar el señor Torres?

....

13. ¿Qué sería mejor que hiciera la señora Gómez antes de darle el dinero a su hijo?

....

Some additional questions:

14. ¿Cree Ud. que sus alumnos aprovechan bien el año escolar?

....

15. Si un alumno llegara tarde, ¿lo dejaría Ud. sin recreo?

....

16. ¿Permitiría Ud. que un niño que no estuviera matriculado asistiera a su clase?

....

17. ¿Les pide Ud. a los padres de sus alumnos que trabajen de voluntarios?

....

18. ¿Cuántos alumnos están matriculados en esta clase?

....

19. ¿Les agradece Ud. a los padres su cooperación?

....

20. ¿Cree Ud. que los maestros reciben un buen sueldo?

....

DIALOGUE COMPLETION

Using your imagination and the vocabulary learned in this lesson, complete the missing lines of this dialogue.

El maestro de quinto grado tiene hoy una reunión con los padres de sus alumnos.

SRA. PAZ —..

MAESTRO —No, es mejor que no llegue demasiado temprano porque entonces no tiene supervisión.

SRA. PAZ —..

MAESTRO —Si Ud. empieza a trabajar muy temprano, podría dejarla en casa de una vecina o una amiga.

SR. LÓPEZ	—..
MAESTRO	—Los niños deben estar en la parada del ómnibus diez minutos antes de la llegada del autobús.
SRA. ROCA	—..
MAESTRO	—Si un niño no viene a clase, debe traer una nota al día siguiente, explicando su ausencia.
SR. DÍAZ	—..
MAESTRO	—¡Qué lástima! Siento mucho que le robaran la bicicleta.
SR. PÉREZ	—..
MAESTRO	—¡Buena idea! Todos los niños deberían tener un candado para la bicicleta.
SRA. GÓMEZ	—..
MAESTRO	—Si Ud. no puede pagar el almuerzo, debe llenar una forma para pedirlo gratis.
SR. ROJAS	—Cambiando de tema… ¿Ud. permite que un niño que no esté matriculado en esta escuela asista a su clase?
MAESTRO	—..
	....
SRA. DÍAZ	—Ud. tiene razón. Eso sería un problema.
MAESTRO	—Muchas gracias por estar aquí con nosotros.

SITUATIONAL EXERCISES

What would you say in the following situation?

You are talking to a group of parents during PTA.   You have to do the following:

1. Ask for their cooperation, so that the children will benefit by and make good use of the school year.
2. Tell them children should not get to school too early, because they don't have (any) supervision.
3. Suggest that children who bring their bicycles have a padlock.
4. Say that many children miss the bus and add that that wouldn't happen if they were at the bus stop early.
5. Tell them that, if a child has a doctor's appointment, he should bring a note from his parents, explaining the reason for being late or for his absence.
6. Advise them that a parent may apply for a cheaper or free lunch, according to his/her salary.
7. Tell them that many children lose their lunch money and suggest that they put lunch money in a sealed envelope before giving it to the child.
8. Ask them to please work as volunteers to help the children.
9. Thank them for coming.

YOU'RE ON YOUR OWN!

With a classmate, act out the following situation.

A principal and a parent are discussing different problems. The principal should explain school regulations and offer solutions.

VOCABULARY EXPANSION (Optional)

Things you might want to say during parent-teacher conference

Su hijo(-a) tiene que
(Your son [daughter] has to)

terminar el trabajo en el tiempo asignado.
(finish the work in the alloted time.)

aprender a respetar la propiedad de otros.
(learn to respect other people's property.)

devolver los libros de la biblioteca.
(return library books.)

asistir a clase regularmente.
(attend class regularly.)

volver a tomar el examen.
(take the exam again.)

repetir el .... grado.
(repeat the .... grade.)

ser más considerado con sus compañeros.
(be more considerate with his/her classmates.)

Su hijo(-a)
(Your son [daughter])

pasa al .... grado.
(is advanced to the .... grade.)

ha mejorado mucho.
(has improved a great deal.)

es muy amistoso(-a).
(is very friendly.)

tiene muchas ideas interesantes.
(has many interesting ideas.)

es muy trabajador(-a)
(is very hard-working.)

es muy popular.
(is very popular.)

es muy inteligente.
(is very intelligent.)

está en el grupo mas adelantado.
(is in the most advanced group.)

Es
(Ha sido)
It is
(It has been)

un placer tener a .... en mi clase.
a pleasure having .... in my class.

Do you remember the expressions used in the Vocabulary Expansion?

This is parent-teacher conference week.   What are you going to say to the parents of these children?

1. *Oscar* misses too many classes and takes library books home and never brings them back.
2. *Elena* always works diligently and is very friendly.
3. *Luis* is very intelligent and is now in the highest reading group.
4. *Alicia* never finishes her work on time, has a tendency to take other children's things and is very inconsiderate.
5. *Teresa* is now doing much better.   She's promoted to the fifth grade.
6. *Ramon* didn't do well in the proficiency test and he might have to be retained in the fourth grade.
7. *Antonio* always contributes interesting ideas during class discussions.   All the other children like him.
8. *Ana* is a child that you enjoy having in your class.

LESSONS 16–20   # VOCABULARY REVIEW

A.   Circle the word or phrase that does not belong in each group.

1. basurero, barras, columpio

2. paz, guerra, arena

3. empujar, observar, vigilar

4. estudio, diámetro, radio

5. muy bien, excelente, mal

6. candado, cita, cerrar

7. cuento, contar, cantar

8. base, dicho, altura

9. concepto, idea, bloque

10. línea, segmento, ancho

11. desgraciadamente, ¡qué lastima!, en realidad

12. ventilación, aire puro, curita

13. personal, individual, colectivo

14. ¡Cuidado!, ¡No te lastimes!, ¡Ven aquí!

15. asiste a clases, viene mañana, está matriculado

B.   Circle the appropriate word or phrase that completes each of the following sentences.

1. En una dieta balanceada necesitamos (carbohidratos, ventilación, hábitos) y proteínas.

2. Para jugar tienen (muñecas, roperos, cuentos) y pelotas.

3. Debe (cepillarse, consumirse, convertirse) los dientes tres veces al día.

4. Es necesario tener buenos hábitos de higiene y nutrición para el mantenimiento de la (grasa, limpieza, salud).

5. Llamamos ángulo a la (altura, abertura, lado) de dos líneas que se cortan.

6. Si comes demasiadas golosinas vas a (engordar, reírte, espiar).

7. Es mejor (permitir, retener, prevenir) que curar.

8. El calcio y el fósforo son minerales (débiles, graciosos, esenciales) para la salud.

9. Esa línea no es horizontal ni vertical, es (nutritiva, inclinada, vacía).

10. El lugar donde se unen los lados de un ángulo se llama (área, vértice, plano).

11. Te voy a (vender, vendar, adivinar) los ojos.

12. Voy a (correr, armar, apagar) la luz.

13. No me puedo (abrochar, parar, enojar) la chaqueta.   Haz el favor de ayudarme.

14. Me (lastimé, quedé, olvidé) de traer los libros.

15. Siéntate aquí, en la alfombra, (según, hacia, al lado) mío.

16. Los niños se portan mal cuando no tienen (punto, tema, supervisión).

17. ¿Quieres tomar una clase en la Universidad? Ve a (beneficiarte, sentarte, matricularte) hoy mismo.

18. Los niños deben formar fila delante (de la razón, de la clase, del sobre).

19. Quiero (solicitar, aprovechar, robar) la oportunidad para hablar con los padres.

20. Si faltó a clase, tiene que traer (una nota, títeres, imaginación) de los padres.

C. **Match the items in column *A* with those in column *B*.**

A

1. ¿Dónde pusiste el rompecabezas? ____

2. ¿Qué vas a preparar para el almuerzo? ____

3. ¿Por qué hay tanto ruido en tu cuarto? ____

4. ¿Tiene un buen sueldo? ____

5. ¿Dónde están tus padres? ____

6. ¿Cómo se llama tu compañero de clase? ____

7. ¿Qué deporte prefieres? ____

8. ¿Dónde tiraste los papeles? ____

9. ¿A quién le toca? ____

10. ¿Qué capítulo estás leyendo? ____

11. ¿Pudiste resolver el problema? ____

12. ¿Son paralelas? ____

13. ¿Crees que tengo razón? ____

14. ¿Sabes contar en español? ____

15. ¿Vas a trabajar de voluntario? ____

16. ¿Qué debo llenar? ____

17. ¿Por qué llegaste tarde? ____

18. ¿Qué tengo que dividir? ____

B

a. En casa.

b. El tercero.

c. A mí.

d. Sí, estoy de acuerdo.

e. No, perpendiculares.

f. No, gana sólo $30 al día.

g. Sí, hasta mil.

h. No, era muy difícil.

i. Carlos Rivas Soto.

j. En la caja.

k. Esta planilla.

l. En el basurero.

m. Porque estoy jugando con los niños.

n. El tenis.

o. Sándwiches y un pastel.

p. Veinte entre cinco.

q. Perdí el omnibus.

r. Sí, porque necesitan mi cooperación.

D. **Crucigrama**

HORIZONTAL

3. opuesto de barato

6. entender

7. lugar donde se pone la ropa

10. adjetivo: ausente; nombre: ____

11. visitar: estar de ____

12. No cuesta nada; es ____

14. opuesto de vertical

17. ¡Vete! ¡Déjame en ____ !

18. lo que hace el médico

19. después

20. forma

22. Vamos a ____ una canción.

23. verbo: llegar; nombre: ____

26. golosina

28. El calcio y el fósforo son ____ muy importantes.

30. La leche tiene ____ D.

32. Están en la ____ del ómnibus.

33. en este momento: ahora ____

34. adjetivo: enfermo; nombre: ____

36. Voy a saltar a la ____ .

38. Para hacer ejercicios, podemos practicar ____ .

40. Él nunca habla; siempre está ____ .

VERTICAL

1. opuesto de *recta*
2. El triángulo y el rectángulo son figuras ____ .
3. perímetro del círculo
4. opuesto de *reír*
5. opuesto de *rápido*
8. Vemos con los ____
9. mineral muy importante
13. Las líneas ____ nunca se encuentran.
15. La usamos para tomar café.
16. dar gracias

20. trozo
21. largo
24. relativo a la escuela
25. Necesitamos proteína para el crecimiento, la reparación y el ____ de los tejidos.
27. verbo: limpiar; nombre: ____
29. Tiene cinco años; va al ____ de infantes.
31. progresar
35. piso
37. permitir

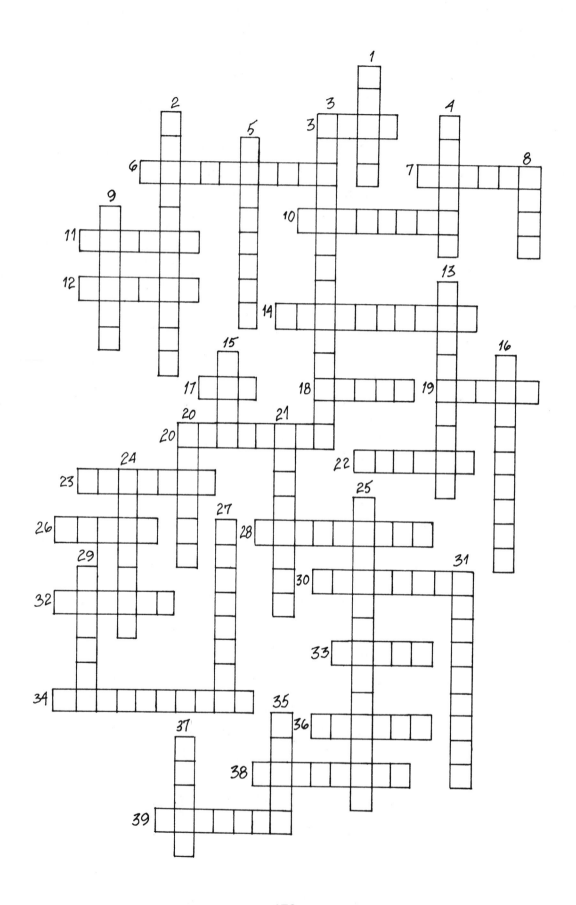

172

Appendixes

Appendix A

Introduction to Spanish Sounds (Recorded on Cassette)

⌨ Each Spanish sound will be explained briefly and examples will be given for practice. Repeat each Spanish word after the speaker, imitating as closely as possible the correct pronunciation.

THE VOWELS

1. The Spanish **a** has a sound similar to the English *a* in the word *father*. Repeat:

   Ana   casa   banana   mala   dama   mata

2. The Spanish **e** is pronounced like the English *e* in the word *eight*. Repeat:

   este   René   teme   deme   entre   bebe

3. The Spanish **i** is pronounced like the English *ee* in the word *see*. Repeat:

   sí   difícil   Mimí   ir   dividir   Fifí

4. The Spanish **o** is similar to the English *o* in the word *no*, but without the glide. Repeat:

   solo   poco   como   toco   con   monólogo

5. The Spanish **u** is similar to the English *ue* sound in the word *Sue*. Repeat:

   Lulú   un   su   universo   murciélago

THE CONSONANTS

1. The Spanish **p** is pronounced like the English *p* in the word *spot*. Repeat:

   pan   papá   Pepe   pila   poco   pude

2. The Spanish **c** in front of **a, o, u, l,** or **r** sounds similar to the English *k*. Repeat:

   casa   como   cuna   clima   crimen   cromo

3. The Spanish **q** is only used in the combinations **que** and **qui** in which the **u** is silent, and also has a sound similar to the English *k*. Repeat:

   que   queso   Quique   quinto   quema   quiso

4. The Spanish **t** is pronounced like the English *t* in the word *stop*. Repeat:

   toma   mata   tela   tipo   atún   Tito

5. The Spanish **d,** at the beginning of an utterance or after **n** or **l,** sounds somewhat similar to the English *d* in the word *David.* Repeat:

día   dedo   duelo   anda   Aldo

In all other positions, the **d** has a sound similar to the English *th* in the word *they.* Repeat:

medida   todo   nada   Ana dice   Eva duda

6. The Spanish **g** also has two sounds. At the beginning of an utterance and in all other positions, except before **e** or **i,** the Spanish **g** sounds similar to the English *g* in the word *sugar.* Repeat:

goma   gato   tengo   lago   algo   aguja

In the combinations **gue** and **gui,** the **u** is silent. Repeat.

Águeda   guineo   guiso   ligue   la guía

7. The Spanish **j,** and **g** before **e** or **i,** sounds similar to the English *h* in the word *home.* Repeat:

jamás   juego   jota   Julio   gente   Genaro   gime

8. The Spanish **b** and the **v** have no difference in sound. Both are pronounced alike. At the beginning of the utterance or after **m** or **n,** they sound similar to the English *b* in the word *obey.* Repeat:

Beto   vaga   bote   vela   también   un vaso

Between vowels, they are pronounced with the lips barely closed. Repeat:

sábado   yo voy   sabe   Ávalos   Eso vale

9. In most Spanish-speaking countries, the **y** and the **ll** are similar to the English *y* in the word *yet.* Repeat:

yo   llama   yema   lleno   ya   lluvia   llega

10. The Spanish **r (ere)** is pronounced like the English *tt* in the word *gutter.* Repeat:

cara   pero   arena   carie   Laredo   Aruba

The Spanish **r** in an initial position and after **l, n,** or **s,** and **rr (erre)** in the middle of a word are pronounced with a strong trill. Repeat:

Rita   Rosa   torre   ruina   Enrique   Israel
perro   parra   rubio   alrededor   derrama

11. The Spanish **s** sound is represented in most of the Spanish-speaking world by the letters **s, z,** and **c** before **e** or **i.** The sound is very similar to the English sibilant *s* in the word *sink.* Repeat:

sale   sitio   solo   seda   suelo
zapato   cerveza   ciudad   cena

In most of Spain, the **z,** and **c** before **e** or **i,** is pronounced like the English *th* in the word *think.* Repeat:

zarzuela   cielo   docena

12. The letter **h** is silent in Spanish. Repeat:

hilo   Hugo   ahora   Hilda   almohada   hermano

13. The Spanish **ch** is pronounced like the English *ch* in the word *chief.* Repeat:

muchacho   chico   coche   chueco   chaparro

14. The Spanish **f** is identical in sound to the English *f.* Repeat:

famoso   feo   difícil   fuego   foto

15. The Spanish **l** is pronounced like the English *l* in the word *lean*. Repeat:

    dolor   ángel   fácil   sueldo   salgo   chaval

16. The Spanish **m** is pronounced like the English *m* in the word *mother*. Repeat:

    mamá   moda   multa   médico   mima

17. In most cases, the Spanish **n** has a sound similar to the English *n*. Repeat:

    nada   norte   nunca   entra   nene

    The sound of the Spanish **n** is often affected by the sounds that occur around it. When it appears before **b, v,** or **p,** it is pronounced like the English *m*. Repeat:

    invierno   tan bueno   un vaso   un bebé   un perro

18. The Spanish **ñ (eñe)** has a sound similar to the English *ny* in the word *canyon*. Repeat:

    muñeca   leña   año   señorita   piña   señor

19. The Spanish **x** has two pronunciations, depending on its position. Between vowels, the sound is similar to the English *ks*. Repeat:

    examen   boxeo   éxito   exigente

    Before a consonant, the Spanish **x** sounds like the English *s*. Repeat:

    expreso   excusa   extraño   exquisito

LINKING

In spoken Spanish, the various words in a phrase or sentence are not pronounced as isolated elements, but are combined. This is called *linking*.

1. The final consonant of a word is pronounced together with the initial vowel of the following word. Repeat:

    Carlos anda   un ángel   el otoño   unos estudiantes

2. The final vowel of a word is pronounced together with the initial vowel of the following word. Repeat:

    su esposo   la hermana   ardua empresa   la invita

3. When the final vowel of a word and the initial vowel of the following word are identical, they are pronounced slightly longer than one vowel. Repeat:

    Ana alcanza   me espera   mi hijo   lo olvida

    The same rule applies when two identical vowels appear within a word. Repeat:

    cooperación   crees   leemos   coordinación

4. When the final consonant of a word and the initial consonant of the following word are the same, they are pronounced as one consonant with slightly longer-than-normal duration. Repeat:

    el lado   un novio   Carlos salta   tienes sed   al leer

177

Appendix B

Spanish Pronunciation

THE ALPHABET

Letter	Name	Letter	Name	Letter	Name	Letter	Name
a	a	g	ge	m	eme	rr	erre
b	be	h	hache	n	ene	s	ese
c	ce	i	i	ñ	eñe	t	te
ch	che	j	jota	o	o	u	u
d	de	k	ka	p	pe	v	ve
e	e	l	ele	q	cu	w	doble ve
f	efe	ll	elle	r	ere	x	equis
						y	y griega
						z	zeta

VOWELS

There are five distinct vowels in Spanish: **a, e, i, o,** and **u.** Each vowel has only one basic, constant sound. The pronunciation of each vowel is constant, clear, and brief. The length of the sound is practically the same whether it is produced in a stressed or unstressed syllable.[1]

While producing the sounds of the English stressed vowels that most closely resemble the Spanish ones, the speaker changes the position of the tongue, lips, and lower jaw, so that the vowel actually starts as one sound and then *glides* into another. In Spanish, however, the tongue, lips, and jaw keep a constant position during the production of the sound.

> **English:** banana   **Spanish:** banana

The stress falls on the same vowel and syllable in both Spanish and English, but the English stressed *a* is longer than the Spanish stressed **a.**

> **English:** banana   **Spanish:** banana

Note also that the English stressed *a* has a sound different from the other *a*'s in the word, while the Spanish **a** sound remains constant.

a in Spanish sounds similar to the English *a* in the word *father.*

alta	casa	palma	Ana
cama	Panamá	alma	apagar

---

[1] In a stressed syllable, the prominence of the vowel is indicated by its loudness.

e is pronounced like the English *e* in the word *eight*.

mes	entre	este	deje
ese	encender	teme	prender

i has a sound similar to the English *ee* in the word *see*.

fin	ir	sí	sin	dividir	Trini	difícil

o is similar to the English *o* in the word *no,* but without the glide.

toco	como	poco	roto
corto	corro	solo	loco

u is pronounced like the English *oo* sound in the word *shoot,* or the *ue* sound in the word *Sue.*

su	Lulú	Úrsula	cultura
un	luna	sucursal	Uruguay

Diphthongs and Triphthongs

When unstressed **i** or **u** falls next to another vowel in a syllable, it unites with that vowel to form what is called a *diphthong*. Both vowels are pronounced as one syllable. Their sounds do not change; they are only pronounced more rapidly and with a glide. For example:

traiga	Lidia	treinta	siete	oigo	adiós
Aurora	agua	bueno	antiguo	ciudad	Luis

A *triphthong* is the union of three vowels: a stressed vowel between two unstressed ones (**i** or **u**) in the same syllable. For example: Paraguay, estudiéis.

NOTE: Stressed **i** and **u** do not form diphthongs with other vowels, except in the combinations **iu** and **ui**. For example: **rí**-o, sa-**bí**-ais.

In syllabication, diphthongs and triphthongs are considered a single vowel; their components cannot be separated.

CONSONANTS

p Spanish **p** is pronounced in a manner similar to the English *p* sound, but without the puff of air that follows after the English sound is produced.

pesca	pude	puedo	parte	papá
postre	piña	puente	Paco	

k The Spanish **k** sound, represented by the letters **k, c** before **a, o, u** or a consonant, and **qu**, is similar to the English *k* sound, but without the puff of air.

casa	comer	cuna	clima	acción	que
quinto	queso	aunque	kiosko	kilómetro	

t Spanish **t** is produced by touching the back of the upper front teeth with the tip of the tongue. It has no puff of air as in the English *t*.

todo	antes	corto	Guatemala	diente
resto	tonto	roto	tanque	

d The Spanish consonant **d** has two different sounds depending on its position. At the beginning of an utterance and after **n** or **l**, the tip of the tongue presses the back of the upper front teeth.

día	doma	dice	dolor	dar
anda	Aldo	caldo	el deseo	un domicilio

In all other positions the sound of **d** is similar to the *th* sound in the English word *they,* but softer.

medida	todo	nada	nadie	medio
puedo	moda	queda	nudo	

g The Spanish consonant **g** is similar to the English *g* sound in the word *guy* except before **e** or **i**.

goma	glotón	gallo	gloria	lago	alga
gorrión	garra	guerra	angustia	algo	Dagoberto

j The Spanish sound **j** (or **g** before **e** and **i**) is similar to a strongly exaggerated English *h* sound.

gemir	juez	jarro	gitano	agente
juego	giro	bajo	gente	

b, v There is no difference in sound between Spanish **b** and **v**. Both letters are pronounced alike. At the beginning of an utterance or after **m** or **n**, **b** and **v** have a sound identical to the English *b* sound in the word *boy*.

vivir	beber	vamos	barco	enviar
hambre	batea	bueno	vestido	

When pronounced between vowels, the Spanish **b** and **v** sound is produced by bringing the lips together but not closing them, so that some air may pass through.

sábado	autobús	yo voy	su barco

y, ll In most countries, Spanish **ll** and **y** have a sound similar to the English sound in the word *yes*.

el llavero	trayecto	su yunta	milla
oye	el yeso	mayo	yema
un yelmo	trayectoria	llama	bella

NOTE: When it stands alone or is at the end of a word, Spanish **y** is pronounced like the vowel **i**.

rey	hoy	y	doy	buey
muy	voy	estoy	soy	

r The sound of Spanish **r** is similar to the English *dd* sound in the word *ladder*.

crema	aroma	cara	arena	aro
harina	toro	oro	eres	portero

rr Spanish **rr** and also **r** in an initial position and after **n, l,** or **s** are pronounced with a very strong trill. This trill is produced by bringing the tip of the tongue near the alveolar ridge and letting it vibrate freely while the air passes through the mouth.

rama	carro	Israel	cierra	roto
perro	alrededor	rizo	corre	Enrique

s   Spanish **s** is represented in most of the Spanish world by the letters **s**, **z**, and **c** before **e** or **i**. The sound is very similar to the English sibilant *s* in the word *sink*.

sale	sitio	presidente	signo
salsa	seda	suma	vaso
sobrino	ciudad	cima	canción
zapato	zarza	cerveza	centro

h   The letter **h** is silent in Spanish.

hoy	hora	hilo	ahora
humor	huevo	horror	almohada

ch   Spanish **ch** is pronounced like the English *ch* in the word *chief*.

hecho	chico	coche	Chile
mucho	muchacho	salchicha	

f   Spanish **f** is identical in sound to the English *f*.

difícil	feo	fuego	forma
fácil	fecha	foto	fueron

l   Spanish **l** is similar to the English *l* in the word *let*.

dolor	lata	ángel	lago	sueldo
los	pelo	lana	general	fácil

m   Spanish **m** is pronounced like the English *m* in the word *mother*.

mano	moda	mucho	muy
mismo	tampoco	multa	cómoda

n   In most cases, Spanish **n** has a sound similar to the English *n*.

nada	nunca	ninguno	norte
entra	tiene	sienta	

The sound of Spanish **n** is often affected by the sounds that occur around it. When it appears before **b**, **v**, or **p**, it is pronounced like an **m**.

tan bueno	toman vino	sin poder
un pobre	comen peras	siguen bebiendo

ñ   Spanish **ñ** is similar to the English *ny* sound in the word *canyon*.

señor	otoño	ñoño	uña
leña	dueño	niños	años

x   Spanish **x** has two pronunciations depending on its position. Between vowels the sound is similar to English *ks*.

examen	exacto	boxeo	éxito
oxidar	oxígeno	existencia	

When it occurs before a consonant, Spanish **x** sounds like *s*.

expresión	explicar	extraer	excusa
expreso	exquisito	extremo	

NOTE: When **x** appears in México or in other words of Mexican origin, it is pronounced like the Spanish letter **j**.

RHYTHM

Rhythm is the variation of sound intensity that we usually associate with music. Spanish and English each regulate these variations in speech differently, because they have different patterns of syllable length. In Spanish the length of the stressed and unstressed syllables remains almost the same, while in English stressed syllables are considerably longer than unstressed ones. Pronounce the following Spanish words, enunciating each syllable clearly.

es-tu-dian-te	bue-no	Úr-su-la
com-po-si-ción	di-fí-cil	ki-ló-me-tro
po-li-cí-a	Pa-ra-guay	

Because the length of the Spanish syllables remains constant, the greater the number of syllables in a given word or phrase, the longer the phrase will be.

LINKING

In spoken Spanish, the different words in a phrase or a sentence are not pronounced as isolated elements but are combined together. This is called *linking*.

Pepe come pan.	→	Pe-pe-co-me-pan
Tomás toma leche.		To-más-to-ma-le-che
Luis tiene la llave.		Luis-tie-ne-la-lla-ve
La mano de Roberto.		La-ma-no-de-Ro-ber-to

1. The final consonant of a word is pronounced together with the initial vowel of the following word.

Carlos anda	→	Car-lo-san-da
un ángel		u-nán-gel
el otoño		e-lo-to-ño
unos estudios interesantes		u-no-ses-tu-dio-sin-te-re-san-tes

2. A diphthong is formed between the final vowel of a word and the initial vowel of the following word. A triphthong is formed when there is a combination of three vowels (see rules for the formation of diphthongs and triphthongs on page 179).

su hermana	→	suher-ma-na
tu escopeta		tues-co-pe-ta
Roberto y Luis		Ro-ber-toy-Luis
negocio importante		ne-go-cioim-por-tan-te
lluvia y nieve		llu-viay-nie-ve
ardua empresa		ar-duaem-pre-sa

3. When the final vowel of a word and the initial vowel of the following word are identical, they are pronounced slightly longer than one vowel.

A-nal-can-za	Ana alcanza	tie-ne-so	tiene eso
lol-vi-do	lo olvido	Ada-tien-de	Ada atiende

The same rule applies when two identical vowels appear within a word.

cres	crees
Te-rán	Teherán
cor-di-na-ción	coordinación

4. When the final consonant of a word and the initial consonant of the following word are the same, they are pronounced as one consonant with slightly longer than normal duration.

    e-*l*a-do   el lado   tie-ne-*s*ed   tienes sed

    Car-lo-*s*al-ta   Carlos salta

INTONATION

Intonation is the rise and fall of pitch in the delivery of a phrase or a sentence. In general, Spanish pitch tends to change less than English, giving the impression that the language is less emphatic.

As a rule, the intonation for normal statements in Spanish starts in a low tone, raises to a higher one on the first stressed syllable, maintains that tone until the last stressed syllable, and then goes back to the initial low tone, with still another drop at the very end.

    Tu amigo viene mañana.   José come pan.

    Ada está en casa.   Carlos toma café.

SYLLABLE FORMATION IN SPANISH

General rules for dividing words into syllables:

Vowels

1. A vowel or a vowel combination can constitute a syllable.

    a-lum-no   a-bue-la   Eu-ro-pa

2. Diphthongs and triphthongs are considered single vowels and cannot be divided.

    bai-le   puen-te   Dia-na   es-tu-diáis   an-ti-guo

3. Two strong vowels (**a, e, o**) do not form a diphthong and are separated into two syllables.

    em-ple-ar   vol-te-ar   lo-a

4. A written accent on a weak vowel (**i** or **u**) breaks the diphthong, thus the vowels are separated into two syllables.

    trí-o   dú-o   Ma-rí-a

Consonants

1. A single consonant forms a syllable with the vowel that follows it.

    po-der   ma-no   mi-nu-to

    NOTE: **ch, ll,** and **rr** are considered single consonants: **a-ma-ri-llo, co-che, pe-rro.**

2. When two consonants appear between two vowels, they are separated into two syllables.

    al-fa-be-to   cam-pe-ón   me-ter-se   mo-les-tia

    EXCEPTION: When a consonant cluster composed of **b, c, d, f, g, p,** or **t** with **l** or **r** appears between two vowels, the cluster joins the following vowel: **so-bre, o-tros, ca-ble, te-lé-gra-fo.**

3. When three consonants appear between two vowels, only the last one goes with the following vowel.

     ins-pec-tor   trans-por-te   trans-for-mar

EXCEPTION: When there is a cluster of three consonants in the combinations described in rule 2, the first consonant joins the preceding vowel and the cluster joins the following vowel: **es-cri-bir, ex-tran-je-ro, im-plo-rar, es-tre-cho.**

ACCENTUATION

In Spanish, all words are stressed according to specific rules. Words that do not follow the rules must have a written accent to indicate the change of stress. The basic rules for accentuation are as follows.

1. Words ending in a vowel, **n,** or **s** are stressed on the next-to-the last syllable.

    hi-jo   **ca**-lle   **me**-sa   fa-**mo**-sos
    flo-**re**-cen   **pla**-ya   **ve**-ces

2. Words ending in a consonant, except **n** or **s,** are stressed on the last syllable.

    ma-**yor**   a-**mor**   tro-pi-**cal**   na-**riz**   re-**loj**   co-rre-**dor**

3. All words that do not follow these rules must have the written accent.

    ca-**fé**   **lá**-piz   **mú**-si-ca   sa-**lón**
    án-gel   **lí**-qui-do   fran-**cés**   **Víc**-tor
    sim-**pá**-ti-co rin-**cón**   a-**zú**-car   **dár**-se-lo
    sa-**lió**   **dé**-bil   e-**xá**-me-nes   **dí**-me-lo

4. Pronouns and adverbs of interrogation and exclamation have a written accent to distinguish them from relative pronouns.

    ¿**Qué** comes?   *What are you eating?*
    La pera que él no comió.   *The pear that he did not eat.*

    ¿**Quién** está ahí?   *Who is there?*
    El hombre a quien tú llamaste. *The man whom you called.*

    ¿**Dónde** está?   *Where is he?*
    En el lugar donde trabaja.   *At the place where he works.*

5. Words that have the same spelling but different meanings take a written accent to differentiate one from the other.

    el *the*   él *he, him*   te *you*   té *tea*
    mi *my*   mí *me*   si *if*   sí *yes*
    tu *your*   tú *you*   mas *but* más *more*

Appendix C

Answer Key to the *Crucigramas*

LESSONS 1–5 *Horizontal:* 1. correcto, 3. goma, 9. minúscula, 10. fuente, 11. escuela, 12. adjetivo, 14. gaveta, 16. área, 18. sustantivo, 20. tijera, 21. oración, 22. colorear, 23. millón, 25. chicle, 27. restar, 28. isla, 29. capital, 30. amarillo, 35. izquierda, 36. incendio, 37. sur, 39. examen, 40. montaña. *Vertical:* 1. continente, 2. geografía, 4. oeste, 5. América, 6. modelo, 7. diccionario, 8. cafeteria, 13. fecha, 15. silencio, 17. estado, 19. Atlántico, 23. mascan, 24. marrón, 26. estambre, 31. limita, 32. bien, 33. país, 34. mañana, 38. río.

LESSONS 6–10 *Horizontal:* 2. masticar, 4. gafas, 5. desayuno, 7. coagular, 8. bránqueas, 10. árboles, 11. naranjo, 14. botánico, 16. respiratorio, 20. timbre, 21. armazón, 22. oxígeno, 25. circulatorio, 27. poco, 28. con. *Vertical:* 1. subirse, 3. escamas, 6. oculista, 8. bajo, 9. anfibio, 12. distinto, 13. vertebral, 17. serpiente, 18. invertebrados, 19. anatomía, 23. grado, 24. piel, 26. todo.

LESSONS 11–15 *Horizontal:* 3. elección, 4. japonés, 7. plural, 8. independencia, 10. recíproco, 11. barato, 12. física, 13. viaje, 15. tierra, 17. esclavitud, 19. fracciones, 21. guerra, 22. Inglaterra, 23. decimal, 24. contestar, 29. medida, 32. concurso, 33. vocal, 34. kilogramo, 35. irregular. *Vertical:* 1. compuesto, 2. gente, 5. presidente, 6. divisible, 9. peregrinos, 14. prosperidad, 16. sobre, 18. yarda, 20. inclinado, 25. dividir, 26. ortografía, 28. tonelada, 30. impropia, 31. uso.

LESSONS 16–20 *Horizontal:* 3. caro, 6. comprender, 7. ropero, 10. ausencia, 11. visita, 12. gratis, 14. horizontal, 17. paz, 18. curar, 19. luego, 20. planilla, 22. cantar, 23. llegada, 26. dulce, 28. minerales, 30. vitamina, 32. parada, 33. mismo, 34. enfermedad, 36. cuerda, 38. deportes, 39. callado. *Vertical:* 1. curva, 2. geométricas, 3. circunferencia, 4. llorar, 5. despacio, 8. ojos, 9. hierro, 13. paralelas, 15. taza, 16. agradecer, 20. pedazo, 21. longitud, 24. escolar, 25. mantenimiento, 27. limpieza, 29. jardín, 31. adelantan, 35. suelo, 37. dejar.

Vocabulary

así like this
 —que so
Asia (*m.*) Asia
asistir to attend
astronomía (*f.*) astronomy
atención (*f.*) attention
Atlántico (*m.*) Atlantic
átomo (*m.*) atom
atrasado(-a) behind
atún (*m.*) tuna fish
aula (*f.*) classroom
aumentar to increase, to go up, to augment
ausencia (*f.*) absence
ausente absent
autobus (*m.*) bus
ave (*f.*) bird, fowl
ayuda (*f.*) help
ayudar to help
azúcar (*f., m.*) sugar
azul blue

B

bajar(se) to get off
bajo(-a) low
bajo under
balanceado(-a) balanced
banana (*f.*) banana
bandera (*f.*) flag
bañar(se) to bathe
baño (*m.*) bathroom, bath
barato(-a) inexpensive, cheap
barras (*f.*) bars
base (*f.*) base
básico(-a) basic
bastar to be enough
basurero (*m.*) trash can
batalla (*f.*) battle
beber to drink
beneficiarse (de) to benefit by
biblioteca (*f.*) library
bien well, correct, okay
blanco(-a) white
bloque (*m.*) block
blusa (*f.*) blouse
boca (*f.*) mouth
bonito(-a) pretty, beautiful
borrador (*m.*) eraser
borrar to erase
branquias (*f.*) branchias
bronquios (*m.*) bronchial tubes
bueno well
bufanda (*f.*) scarf
bulla (*f.*) noise
buscar to look up, to look for

C

caballo (*m.*) horse
cabello (*m.*) hair
cabeza (*f.*) head
cabo (*m.*) cape
cabra (*f.*) goat
cactus (*m.*) cactus
cada each
café brown
cafetería (*f.*) cafeteria
caja (*f.*) box
cajón (*m.*) drawer
calcar to trace
calcetín (*m.*) sock
calcio (*m.*) calcium
cálido(-a) warm, hot
caliente hot
calor (*m.*) heat
callado(-a) quiet, silent
callarse to be quiet
cambiar to change
cambio (*m.*) change
camelia (*f.*) camellia
camello (*m.*) camel
caminar to walk
camisa (*f.*) shirt
camiseta (*f.*) T-shirt
candado (*m.*) padlock
cangrejo crab
centena (*f.*) hundred
centésima (*f.*) hundredth
centímetro (*m.*) centimeter
cepillar(se) to brush
cerebelo (*m.*) cerebellum
cerebro (*m.*) brain
cereza (*f.*) cherry
cerrar (e:ie) to close, to shut
ciclón (*m.*) cyclone
ciencia (*f.*) science
 —sociales Social Sciences
científico(-a) scientific
cifra (*f.*) cipher
cilindro (*m.*) cylinder
cinto (*m.*) belt
cinturón (*m.*) belt
círculo (*m.*) circle
circunferencia (*f.*) circumference
cita (*f.*) appointment
civil civil
ciudad (*f.*) city
claro (-a) clear, light
clase (*f.*) kind, type, class
clavel (*m.*) carnation
clima (*m.*) climate
cloro (*m.*) chlorine

coagular to coagulate
cociente (*m.*) quotient
cocina (*f.*) kitchen
cocodrilo (*m.*) crocodile
codo (*m.*) elbow
col (*f.*) cabbage
colonia (*f.*) colony
colonizar to colonize
colorear to color
columna vertebral (*f.*) spine
columpio (*m.*) swing
coma (*f.*) comma
combinación (*f.*) combination
comenzar (e:ie) to begin, to start
comer to eat
cómico(-a) funny
comida (*f.*) food
comillas (*f.*) quotation marks
cómo how
compañero(-a) de clase classmate
compás (*m.*) compass
complemento (*m.*) object
componer to compose, to be found in
composición (*f.*) composition
comprender to understand
comprensión (*f.*) comprehension
comprobar (o:ue) to verify
compuesto(-a) compound
común common
comunismo (*m.*) communism
con with
concepto (*m.*) concept
concurso (*m.*) contest
 —de ortografía (*m.*) spelling bee
condensación (*f.*) condensation
conducta (*f.*) citizenship, conduct, behavior
conejo(-a) rabbit
congreso (*m.*) congress
conjunción (*f.*) conjunction
cono (*m.*) cone
conocimiento (*m.*) knowledge
conquistador (*m.*) conqueror
consonante (*f.*) consonant
constelación (*f.*) constellation
constitución (*f.*) constitution
consumir to consume
contar (o:ue) to count, to tell
contento(-a) happy, contented
contestar to answer
continente (*m.*) continent
continuar to continue

contra against
contracción (*f.*) contraction
conversación (*f.*) conversation
convertirse (en) (e:ie) to turn into
copiar to copy
cooperación (*f.*) cooperation
corazón (*m.*) heart
corchetes (*m.*) brackets
cordillera (*f.*) cordillera, chain of mountains
correcto(-a) correct
corregir (e:i) to correct
correr to run
cortar to cut
cosa (*f.*) thing
coser to sew
costa (*f.*) coast
coyuntura (*f.*) joint
cráneo (*m.*) skull
crecimiento (*m.*) growing
cuaderno (*m.*) notebook
cuadrado(-a) square
cuál(es) which, what
cuando when
cuántos (-as) how many
cuarto (*m.*) room, fourth, quart
cúbico(-a) cubic
cubierto(-a) (de) covered (with)
cubrir to cover
cucaracha (*f.*) cockroach
cuello (*m.*) neck
cuenta (*f.*) math problem
cuento (*m.*) story, short story
cuerda (*f.*) rope
cuerpo (*m.*) body
cuidado (*m.*) care
¡cuidado! look out!
curar to cure
curita (*f.*) bandaid
curvo (-a) curved

CH

chaqueta (*f.*) jacket
chica girl
chicle (*m.*) chewing gum
chico boy
chile (*m.*) pepper, chili

D

dar to give
de arriba top, upper
de quien whose

debajo (de) under
deber must, should
débil weak
década (*f.*) decade
decena (*f.*) denary
décima (*f.*) tenth
decimal decimal
decímetro (*m.*) decimeter
decir (e:i) to say, to tell
declarar to declare
dedo (*m.*) finger
  —del pie (*m.*) toe
definición (*f.*) definition
dejar to let, to allow, to leave behind
  —en paz to leave alone
delante (de) in front of
demás other, rest
demasiado(-a) too, too much
democracia (*f.*) democracy
denominador (*m.*) denominator
dentro in, inside
depender to depend
depresión (*f.*) depression
derecho(a) right
derrotar to defeat
desayuno (*m.*) breakfast
descubrir to discover
desdoblar unfold
desgraciadamente unfortunately
desierto (*m.*) desert
despacio slowly
después (de) after
detrás (de) behind
devolver (o:ue) to return, to give back
día (*m.*) day
diámetro (*m.*) diameter
dibujar to draw
dibujo (*m.*) drawing
diccionario (*m.*) dictionary
dictado (*m.*) dictation
dicho (*m.*) saying
diente (*m.*) tooth
dieta (*f.*) diet
diferencia (*f.*) difference
diferente different
digerir (e:ie) to digest
digestión (*f.*) digestion
director(-a) principal, director
disco (*m.*) record
disminuir to diminish, to decrease, to go down
disolver (o:ue) to dissolve
distinto(-a) different

dividendo (*m.*) dividend
dividir to divide
divisible divisible
división (*m.*) division
divisor divisor
doblado(-a) folded
doblar to fold, to double
doméstico(-a) domestic
domicilio (*m.*) address
dónde where
dos puntos colon
dulce (*m.*) sweet
durante during
durar to last

E

educación física (*f.*) physical education
ejemplo (*m.*) example
ejercicio (*m.*) exercise
elección (*f.*) election
electricidad (*f.*) electricity
electrón (*m.*) electron
elefante (*m.*) elephant
elegir (e:i) to elect, to choose, to select
elemento (*m.*) element
empezar (e:ie) to begin, to start
empujar to push
en on, in, at
  —casa at home
  —realidad in fact
  —voz alta aloud
encender (e:ie) to turn on
encima de on top of
encontrar (o:ue) to find
encontrarse (o:ue) to meet (each other)
energía (*f.*) energy
enfermedad (*f.*) disease
enfermero(-a) nurse
enfermo(-a) sick, ill
engordar to get fat
enojarse to get angry
enseñar to teach
entender (e:ie) to understand
entero (*m.*) whole
entrar (en) to enter
entre between, among, by (in division)
entregar to turn in
enviar to send
época (*f.*) time
equilátero equilateral
equivalencia (*f.*) equivalence

escaleno   scalene
escama (f.)   scale
esclavitud (f.)   slavery
esclavo(a)   slave
escolar   school
escribir   to write
escritorio (m.)   desk
escuchar   to listen
escuela (f.)   school
esencial   essential
esfera (f.)   sphere
esforzarse (o:ue)   to try, to
   make an effort
esfuerzo (m.)   effort
esófago (m.)   esophagus
espacio (m.)   space
espalda (f.)   back
España   Spain
espejuelos (m.)   eyeglasses
esperar   to wait
espiar   to peek, to spy
esqueleto (m.)   skeleton
esquina (f.)   corner
establecido(-a)   established
estación (f.)   season
estado (m.)   state
Estados Unidos   United States
estambre (m.)   yarn
estante (m.)   shelf
este (m.)   East
estómago (m.)   stomach
estrella (f.)   star
estudiar   to study
estudio (m.)   study
Europa (f.)   Europe
evaporación (f.)   evaporation
exactamente   exactly
examen (m.)   exam
excelente   excellent
excepción (f.)   exception
excepto   except
excursión (f.)   field trip
existir   to exist
explicar   to explain

F

fácil   easy
factor (m.)   factor
falda (f.)   skirt
faltar   to miss
fecha (f.)   date
fieltro (m.)   felt
figura (f.)   figure
fila (f.)   line
filtrar   to filter
final   final
firmar   to sign

física (f.)   physics
flor (f.)   flower
forma (f.)   shape, form
formar   to form
formarse fila   to line up
fórmula (f.)   formula
fósforo (m.)   phosphorus
fotografía (f.)   photograph
fracción (f.)   fraction
   —impropia (f.)   improper
   fraction
   —propia (f.)   proper fraction
   —común (f.)   common
   fraction
Francia (f.)   France
frente   front
fresa (f.)   strawberry
frío(-a)   cold
fuego (m.)   fire
fuente (f.)   source
fundar   to found
futuro (m.)   future

G

gafas (f.)   eyeglasses
galón (m.)   gallon
gallina (f.)   hen
gallo (m.)   rooster
ganadería (f.)   livestock
gaseoso(-a)   gaseous
gato(-a)   cat
gaveta (f.)   drawer
generalmente   generally
gente (f.)   people
geografía (f.)   geography
geometría (f.)   geometry
geométrico(a)   geometric
gladiolo (m.)   gladiolus
glándula (f.)   gland
   —anexa (f.)   annexed gland
   —salivales (f.)   salivary
   glands
globo terráqueo (m.)   globe
glóbulo (m.)   corpuscle
   —rojo (m.)   red corpuscle
gobernador(-a)   governor
gobierno (m.)   government
golfo (m.)   gulf
golosina (f.)   sweet
goma de mascar (f.)   chewing
   gum
goma de pegar (f.)   glue
gracioso(-a)   funny
grado (m.)   degree, grade
gramo (m.)   gram
grande   large, big
grasa (f.)   fat

gratis   free (of charge)
gris   gray
grupo (m.)   group
guante (m.)   glove
guardar   to put away, to keep
guerra (f.)   war
guión (m.)   hyphen
gusto (m.)   taste, sense of taste

H

habilidad (f.)   ability
habitante (m.,f.)   inhabitant
hábito (m.)   habit
hablar   to speak
hacer   to do, to make
hacer un viaje   to take a trip
hacia   toward
hallar   to find
hasta   until
hermana   sister
hermano   brother
hexágono (m.)   hexagon
hidrógeno (m.)   hydrogen
hierro (m.)   iron
higado (m.)   liver
higiene (f.)   hygiene
hija   daughter
hijo   son
hilo (m.)   thread
hipopótamo (m.)   hippo-
   potamus
historia (f.)   history
hoja (f.)   leaf
Holanda   Holland
hora (f.)   time, hour
   —de salida   quitting time
horizontal   horizontal
hormiga (f.)   ant
hoy   today
hueso (m.)   bone
huevo (m.)   egg
huracán (m.)   hurricane

I

imaginación (f.)   imagination
impar   odd (number)
impermeable (m.)   raincoat
incendio (m.)   fire
inclinado(-a)   inclined
incluido(-a)   included
independencia (f.)   independence
independientemente   independently
indios (m.)   Indians

industria (*f.*) industry
Inglaterra England
inorgánico(-a) inorganic
insecto (*m.*) insect
instrucción (*f.*) instruction
inteligente intelligent
interjección (*f.*) interjection
intestino (*m.*) intestine
—**delgado** (*m.*) small
   intestine
—**grueso** (*m.*) large intestine
invertebrado invertebrate
ir to go
irregular irregular
isla (*f.*) island
isósceles isosceles
izquierdo(-a) left

J

Japón (*m.*) Japan
japonés(-esa) Japanese
jardín (*m.*) garden
—**botánico** (*m.*) botanical
   garden
—**infantes** (*m.*)
   kindergarten
jirafa (*f.*) giraffe

K

kilogramo (*m.*) kilo, kilogram
kilómetro (*m.*) kilometer
kindergarten (*m.*) kindergarten

L

lado (*m.*) side
lagartija (*f.*) lizard
lago (*m.*) lake
lámina (*f.*) picture, illustration
lana de tejer (*f.*) yarn
langosta (*f.*) lobster
largo(-a) long, length
lápiz (*m.*) pencil
lastimar(se) to hurt, to get hurt
lectura (*f.*) reading
—**oral** oral reading
leche (*f.*) milk
lechuga (*f.*) lettuce
lengua (*f.*) tongue
lenguaje (*m.*) language
lentes (*m.*) eyeglasses
león (-ona) lion
letra (*f.*) letter, handwriting
levantar to raise
ley (*f.*) law

libra (*f.*) pound
liberar to free, to liberate
librarse (de) to be (become)
   free (from)
libre free
libreta de calificaciones (*f.*)
   report card
libro (*m.*) book
limitar (con) to border (with)
límite (*m.*) boundary
limón (*m.*) lemon
limpiar to clean
limpieza (*f.*) cleanliness
línea (*f.*) line
—**de puntos** (*f.*) dotted line
lineal linear
líquido(-a) liquid
lista (*f.*) list
listo(-a) ready
litro (*m.*) liter
lo que what
longitud (*f.*) length
luego then, later
luna (*f.*) moon
luz (*f.*) light
—**del sol** (*f.*) sunlight

Ll

llamar to call
llamarse to be called
llegada (*f.*) arrival
llegar to arrive
—**tarde** to be late
llenar to fill
llevar to take, to carry
llorar to cry
lloviznar to drizzle

M

madre mother
maestro(-a) teacher
mal badly, wrong
mamá Mom
mamífero (*m.*) mammal
mano (*f.*) hand
mantener(se) to keep
   oneself), to maintain
mantenimiento (*m.*)
   maintenance
manzana (*f.*) apple
mañana tomorrow
mapa (*m.*) map
máquina (*f.*) machine
mar (*m.*) sea
margarita (*f.*) daisy

mariposa (*f.*) butterfly
marrón brown
más (*f.*) plus (+), more
mascar to chew
masticar to chew
matemáticas math
materia (*f.*) matter
material (*m.*) material
matriculado(-a) enrolled,
   registered
matricularse to enroll, to
   register
mayor bigger, larger, older,
   oldest
mayúscula capital (letter)
medias (*f.*) stockings
medida (*f.*) measure,
   measurement
—**cuadrada** (*f.*) square
   measure
—**de capacidad** (*f.*) liquid
   measure
—**de longitud** (*f.*) lineal
   measure
—**de peso** (*f.*) weight
   measure
—**lineal** (*f.*) lineal
   measure
medio(-a) half
medir (e:i) to measure
médula espinal (*f.*) spinal
   cord
mejor better
mejorar to improve
menor smaller, younger
menos (−) minus
meridiano (*m.*) meridian
mesa (*f.*) table
metro (*m.*) meter
mezcla (*f.*) mixture
microbio (*m.*) germ
milímetro (*m.*) milimeter
milla (*f.*) mile
millón (*m.*) million
mina (*f.*) mine
mineral (*m.*) mineral
minuendo (*m.*) minuend
minúscula small (letter)
mismo(-a) same
mitad (*f.*) half
mixto(-a) mixed
modelo (*m.*) pattern
molécula (*f.*) molecule
monarquía (*f.*) monarchy
mono(-a) monkey
montaña (*f.*) mountain
monte (*m.*) mount

morado(-a) purple
mosca (*f.*) fly
mosquito (*m.*) mosquito
mover (o:ue) to move
mucho(-a) much
mudo(-a) silent
multiplicación (*f.*)
multiplication
multiplicador (*m.*) multiplier
multiplicando (*m.*)
multiplicand
multiplicar to multiply
múltiplo (*m.*) multiple
mundial world, worldwide
mundo (*m.*) world
muñeca (*f.*) doll
músculo (*m.*) muscle
música (*f.*) music

N

nacer to be born
naranja (*f.*) orange
naranjo (*m.*) orange tree
nariz (*f.*) nose
naturaleza (*f.*) nature
Navidad (*f.*) Christmas
necesario(-a) necessary
negro(-a) black
nervio (*m.*) nerve
neutral neutral
neutrón (*m.*) neutron
niña girl, child
niño boy, child
niños(-as) children
nivel (*m.*) level
nombrar to name
nombre (*m.*) noun
—**común** (*m.*) common noun
—**propio** (*m.*) proper noun
norte (*m.*) North
nota (*f.*) note
nuevo(-a) new
numerador (*m.*) numerator
número (*m.*) number
nunca never
nutrición (*f.*) nutrition
nutritivo(-a) nourishing

O

observar to observe
obtuso obtuse
océano (*m.*) ocean
octágono (*m.*) octagon
oculista (*m., f.*) opthalmologist
ocurrir to happen

oeste (*m.*) West
oficina (*f.*) office
oído (*m.*) inner ear, sense of
hearing
ojo (*m.*) eye
olfato (*m.*) sense of smell
olvidar (se) (de) to forget
ómnibus (*m.*) bus
onda corta (*f.*) short wave
onda larga (*f.*) long wave
onza (*f.*) ounce
operación (*f.*) operation
operar to operate
oración (*f.*) sentence
orgánico(-a) organic
órgano (*m.*) organ
orquídea (*f.*) orchid
ortografía (*f.*) spelling
oscuro(-a) dark
otra vez again
otro(-a) other, another
oveja (*f.*) sheep
oxígeno (*m.*) oxygen

P

Pacífico (*m.*) Pacific
padre father
padres parents
página (*f.*) page
país (*m.*) country, nation
pájaro (*m.*) bird
palabra (*f.*) word
palanca (*f.*) lever
páncreas (*m.*) pancreas
pantalón (*m.*) pants
papa (*f.*) potato
papá Dad, father
papel (*m.*) paper
par even (number)
para for
paralelo(-a) parallel
paralelogramo (*m.*)
parallelogram
pararse to stand, to stand up
paréntesis (*m.*) parentheses
parte (*f.*) part
participar to participate
pasado past
pasar to spend time, to pass,
to go, to happen
paso (*m.*) step
pastel (*m.*) pie
patata (*f.*) potato
patio (*m.*) backyard
pato(-a) duck
patrón (*m.*) pattern, model

pavo(-a) turkey
paz (*f.*) peace
pecho (*m.*) chest
pedazo (*m.*) piece
pedir (e:i) to ask (for), to
request, to order
—**prestado** to borrow
—**turno** to make an
appointment
pegar to glue, to hit
pelear (se) to fight
película (*f.*) film, movie
pelo (*m.*) hair
pelota (*f.*) ball
península (*f.*) peninsula
pensamiento (*m.*) pansy
pensar (e:ie) to think
pentágono (*m.*) pentagon
pequeño(-a) small, little
pera (*f.*) pear
perder (e:ie) to miss, to lose
peregrino(-a) pilgrim
perímetro (*m.*) perimeter
permitir to allow, to let, to
permit
pero but
perpendicular perpendicular
persecución (*f.*) persecution
persona (*f.*) person
personal personal
pertenecer to belong
perro(-a) dog
pesca (*f.*) fishing
pez (*m.*) fish
pico (*m.*) beak
pie (*m.*) foot
piel (*f.*) skin
pigmento (*m.*) pigment
pila (*f.*) battery
pincel (*m.*) brush
pinta (*f.*) pint
pintar to color, to paint
pintura (*f.*) paint, painting
piña (*f.*) pineapple
pionero(-a) pioneer
pirámide (*f.*) pyramid
piso (*m.*) floor
pizarra (*f.*) blackboard
pizarrón (*m.*) blackboard
planeta (*m.*) planet
planilla (*f.*) form
plano (*m.*) plane
—**inclinado** (*m.*) inclined
plane
planta (*f.*) plant
plaqueta (*f.*) blood platelet
plátano (*m.*) banana

pluma (*f.*)   feather, pen
plural   plural
población (*f.*)   population
poco (*m.*)   little (*ref. to quantity*)
poder (o:ue)   to be able to, can
polea (*f.*)   pulley
polígono (*m.*)   polygon
polo (*m.*)   pole
pomelo (*m.*)   grapefruit
poner   to put
ponerse en fila   to line up
por ciento   per cent
¿por qué?   why?
porque   because
portarse   to behave
potencia (*f.*)   power
práctica (*f.*)   drill
precedido   preceded
predicado(a) (*m.*)   predicate
prefijo (*m.*)   prefix
prender   to turn on
preparar(se)   to prepare
   (oneself), to get ready
preposición (*f.*)   preposition
presente   present
presidente (*m.*)   president
prestar atención   to pay
   attention
prevenir   to prevent
primero(-a)   first
primo   prime
principal   main
principalmente   mainly
problema (*m.*)   problem
producto (*m.*)   product
pronto   soon
pronunciar   to pronounce
propiedades (*f.*)   properties
prosperidad (*f.*)   prosperity
proteger   to protect
protegido(-a)   protected
proteína (*f.*)   protein
protón (*m.*)   proton
próximo(-a)   next
puerta (*f.*)   door
pulgada (*f.*)   inch
pulmón (*m.*)   lung
punto (*m.*)   period, point
punto y coma (*m.*)   semicolon
purificar   purify
puritano(a) (*m.*)   puritan

Q

¿qué?   what?
que   that, what

quebrado (*m.*)   fraction
—**impropio** (*m.*)   improper
fraction
—**propio** (*m.*)   proper
fraction
quedarse   to stay, to remain
quién(es)   who, (plural)
quizá(s)   maybe, perhaps

R

radio (*m.*)   radius
raíz (*f.*)   root
rana (*f.*)   frog
razón (*f.*)   reason
receso (*m.*)   recess
recíproco (*m.*)   reciprocal
recoger (**yo recojo**)   to pick up
recordar (o:ue)   to remember
recortar   to cut, to trim
recreo (*m.*)   recess
rectángulo (*m.*)   rectangle
recto(-a)   straight
reducir   to reduce
regla (*f.*)   rule, ruler
regresar   to return, to go
   (come) back
regular   regular
reino (*m.*)   kingdom
reír(se)   to laugh
religioso(-a)   religious
renacuajo (*m.*)   tadpole
reparación (*f.*)   repair
repasar   to review
repaso (*m.*)   review
repollo (*m.*)   cabbage
representante (*m., f.*)
   Congressman (woman)
reptil (*m.*)   reptile
residuo (*m.*)   remainder
resolver (o:ue)   to solve
respirar   to breathe
respuesta (*f.*)   answer
restar   to subtract
resta (*f.*)   subtraction
resto (*m.*)   difference
retener   to retain
revisar   to check
río (*m.*)   river
rimar   to rhyme
riqueza (*f.*)   wealth
robar   to steal
rodilla (*f.*)   knee
romano(-a)   Roman
rombo (*m.*)   rhomb
romboide (*m.*)   rhomboid

rompecabezas (*m.*)   puzzle
ropa (*f.*)   clothes
ropero (*m.*)   closet
rosa (*f.*)   rose
rosado(-a)   pink
ruido (*m.*)   noise

S

saber   to know
sacapuntas (*m.*)   pencil
   sharpener
sal (*f.*)   salt
salir   to go out
saltar   to jump
—**la cuerda**   to jump rope
salud (*f.*)   health
saludar   to salute, to greet
salvaje (*m., f.*)   wild
sangre (*f.*)   blood
satélite (*m.*)   satellite
satisfactorio(-a)   satisfactory
secretario(-a)   secretary
segmento (*m.*)   segment
seguro(-a)   sure
semilla (*f.*)   seed
senador(-a)   senator
sentar(se) (e:ie)   to sit
sentido (*m.*)   sense
separar(se)   to separate
serpiente (*f.*)   snake, serpent
si   if
siempre   always
siglo (*m.*)   century
significado (*m.*)   meaning
significar   to mean, to signify
signo (*m.*)   sign
—**de admiración** (*m.*)
   exclamation mark
—**de interrogación**   question
mark
sílaba (*f.*)   syllable
silencio (*m.*)   silence
silla (*f.*)   chair
símbolo (*m.*)   symbol
simple   simple
simplificar   to simplify
sin   without
—**falta**   without fail
—**sonido**   silent
singular   singular
sinónimo   synonym
sistema   system
—**sistema de numeración**
   numbering system
—**métrico**   metric system
—**nervioso**   nervous
system

situado(-a) situated, located
sobre (*m.*) envelope
sobre about
sobresaliente outstanding
sodio (*m.*) sodium
sol (*m.*) sun
solamente only
solar solar
solicitar to apply (for)
solidificación (*f.*) solidification
sólido(-a) solid
sólo only, solely
solución (*f.*) solution
sombrear to shade
sonar (o:ue) to ring
sonido (*m.*) sound
sostener to support, to hold
subir(se) to get on
subrayar to underline
sueldo (*m.*) salary
suelo (*m.*) floor
sufijo (*m.*) suffix
sujeto (*m.*) subject
suma (*f.*) total
sumando (*m.*) addend
sumar to add, to add up
suma (*f.*) addition
superficie (*f.*) area
supervisión (*f.*) supervision
suponer to suppose
sur (*m.*) South
sustancia (*f.*) matter
sustantivo (*m.*) noun
sustraendo (*m.*) subtrahend

T

tabla (*f.*) table
tacto (*m.*) sense of touch
tallo (*m.*) stem
también also
tanto(-a) so much
tarde late
tarea (*f.*) homework
taza (*f.*) cup
tejido (*m.*) tissue
teléfono (*m.*) telephone
televisor (*m.*) T.V. set
tema (*m.*) subject, topic
templado(-a) temperate
tenis (*m.*) tennis
terminado(-a) finished

terminar to finish
terremoto (*m.*) earthquake
territorio (*m.*) territory
tiempo (*m.*) time
Tierra (*f.*) Earth
tierra (*f.*) soil, earth, land
—**cultivable** farmland
tigre (*m.*) tiger
tijera(s) (*f.*) scissors
timbre (*m.*) bell
tío uncle
tipo (*m.*) type
tirar to throw
títere (*m.*) puppet
tiza (*f.*) chalk
tobillo (*m.*) ankle
tocadiscos (*m.*) record player
tocarle a uno to be one's turn
todavía still
—**no** not yet
todo(-a) all
todos (-as) all, everybody
tomar to take, to drink
tomarse de las manos to hold
hands
torno (*m.*) winch
tonelada (*f.*) ton
toronja (*f.*) grapefruit
tortuga (*f.*) turtle
total (*m.*) total
trabajar to work
trabajo (*m.*) work
—**manual** arts and crafts
traer to bring
tragar to swallow
transformar to turn into,
to transform
tráquea (*f.*) windpipe, trachea
tratar(de) to try
tratarse de to be about
trazar to draw (i.e., a line)
triángulo (*m.*) triangle
tronco (*m.*) tree, trunk
trozo (*m.*) piece
turno (*m.*) appointment, turn

U

último(-a) last
único(-a) only
unidad (*f.*) unit
unión (*f.*) joining together

unir to unit, to join
usar to use
uso use
uva (*f.*) grape
¡uy! wow!

V

vaca (*f.*) cow
vacaciones (*f.*) vacation
vacío(-a) empty
valer to be worth
varios(-as) several, various
vasos capilares (*m.*) capillary
vessel
vegetal (*m.*) vegetable
velocidad (*f.*) speed, velocity
vena (*f.*) vein
vencer to defeat
venir to come
ventana (*f.*) window
ventilación (*f.*) ventilation
verbo (*m.*) verb
¿verdad? right?, true?
vertebrado vertebrate
vertical vertical
vértice (*m.*) vertix
vestido (*m.*) dress
vez (*f.*) time (in a series)
Vía Láctea (*f.*) Milky Way
viaje (*m.*) trip, journey
vicedirector(-a) vice-principal
vida (*f.*) life
vigilar to watch
violeta (*f.*) violet
vista (*f.*) sight, eyes
vitamina (*f.*) vitamin
vivir to life
vivo(-a) alive
vocabulario (*m.*) vocabulary
vocal (*f.*) vowel
voluntario(-a) volunteer

Y

ya already
yarda (*f.*) yard

Z

zanahoria (*f.*) carrot
zoología (*f.*) zoology

A

abbreviate abreviar
abbreviation abreviatura (*f.*)
ability habilidad (*f.*)
abolish abolir
about acerca de, de, sobre
absence ausencia (*f.*)
accented acentuado(-a)
according to según
acre acre (*m.*)
acute agudo(-a)
add sumar, agregar, añadir
addend sumando (*m.*)
addition suma (*f.*)
address domicilio (*m.*),
   dirección (*f.*)
adjective adjetivo (*m.*)
adverb adverbio (*m.*)
Africa África (*m.*)
after después (de)
again otra vez, de nuevo
against contra
agriculture agricultura (*f.*)
air aire (*m.*)
alive vivo(-a)
all todo(-a), todos (-as)
allies aliados (-as)
allow dejar, permitir
aloud en voz alta
alphabet alfabeto (*m.*)
already ya
also también
always siempre
among entre
amphibian anfibio (*m.*)
anatomy anatomía (*f.*)
angle ángulo (*m.*)
animal animal (*m.*)
ankle tobillo (*m.*)
annexed anexo(-a)
   —glands glándulas anexas
another otro(-a)
answer contestar, contestación
   (*f.*), respuesta (*f.*)
ant hormiga (*f.*)
antonym antónimo (*m.*)
any alguno(-a), cualquier
appear aparecer
apple manzana (*f.*)
apply solicitar
appointment cita (*f.*),
   turno (*m.*)
apostrophe apóstrofe (*m.*)
arabic arábigo(-a)

archipielago archipiélago (*m.*)
area área (*f.*), superficie (*f.*)
arithmetic aritmética (*f.*)
around alrededor (de)
arrival llegada (*f.*)
arrive llegar
art arte (*m.*)
artery arteria (*f.*)
Asia Asia
ask *(for)* pedir (e:i)
astronomy astronomía (*f.*)
at en, a
at home en casa
Atlantic Atlántico
atom átomo (*m.*)
attend asistir (-a)
attention atención
augment aumentar

B

back espalda (*f.*)
backyard patio (*m.*)
badly mal
balance balancear
balanced balanceado(-a)
ball pelota (*f.*)
banana banana (*f.*), plátano
   (*m.*)
bandaid curita (*f.*)
bars barras (*f.*)
base base (*f.*)
basic básico(-a)
bathe bañar(se)
bathroom baño (*m.*), cuarto
   de baño (*m.*), excusado (*m.*)
   (*Mex.*)
battery pila (*f.*)
battle batalla (*f.*)
be ser, estar
   —about tratarse de
   —enough bastar
   —(become) free from
   librarse (de)
   —late llegar tarde
   —worth valer
beak pico (*m.*)
beautiful hermoso(-a),
   bonito(-a)
because porque
bee abeja (*f.*)
begin comenzar (e:ie),
   empezar (e:ie)
behave portarse

behind atrasado(-a),
   detrás (de)
bell timbre (*m.*), campana
   (*f.*)
belong pertenecer
benefit beneficiar(se),
   beneficio (*m.*)
beside al lado (de)
besides además (de)
better mejor
between entre
big grande
bigger mayor, más grande
bird pájaro (*m.*), ave (*f.*)
black negro(-a)
blackboard pizarra (*f.*),
   pizarrón (*m.*)
block bloque (*m.*), cuadra (*f.*)
blood sangre (*f.*)
   —platelet plaqueta (*f.*)
blue azul
body cuerpo (*m.*)
book libro (*m.*)
bone hueso (*m.*)
border limitar (con), límite
   (*m.*), frontera (*f.*)
born nacido(-a)
borrow pedir prestado(-a)
botanical garden jardín
   botánico (*m.*)
boundary límite (*m.*)
box caja (*f.*)
boy chico, muchacho, niño
bracket corchete (*m.*)
brain cerebro (*m.*)
branchias bránquias (*f.*)
breakfast desayuno (*m.*)
breathe respirar
bring traer
bronchial tubes bronquios (*m.*)
brother hermano
brown marrón, café
brush pincel (*m.*), cepillo (*m.*),
   cepillar(se)
bus autobús (*m.*), ómnibus
   (*m.*), camión (*m.*) (*Mex.*)
   —stop parada (*f.*) de
   ómnibus
but pero
butterfly mariposa (*f.*)
button botón (*m.*)

C

cabbage repollo (*m.*), col (*m.*)

cabinet armario (*m.*)
cactus cactus (*m.*)
cafeteria cafetería (*f.*)
calcium calcio (*m.*)
call llamar, llamada (*f.*)
camel camello (*m.*)
camellia camelia (*f.*)
cape cabo (*m.*)
capillary vessels vasos (*m.*)
  capilares
capital capital (*f.*)
capital (*letter*) mayúscula (*f.*)
capitalism capitalismo (*m.*)
carbohydrate carbohidrato
  (*m.*)
cardboard cartón (*m.*)
care cuidado (*m.*)
carnation clavel (*m.*)
carpet alfombra (*f.*)
carrot zanahoria (*f.*)
carry llevar, cargar
cat gato(-a)
celery apio (*m.*)
centimeter centímetro (*m.*)
central central
Central America América
  Central
century siglo (*m.*)
cerebellum cerebro (*m.*)
chain cadena (*f.*)
  —**of mountains** cordillera
    (*f.*)
chair silla (*f.*)
chalk tiza (*f.*)
change cambiar, cambio (*m.*)
chapter capítulo (*m.*)
characteristic característica
  (*f.*)
cheap barato(-a)
check revisar, chequear,
  cheque (*m.*)
cherry cereza (*f.*)
chest pecho (*m.*)
chew masticar, mascar
chewing gum goma (*f.*) de
  mascar, chicle (*m.*)
child niño(-a)
chlorine cloro (*m.*)
choose elegir (e:i), escoger
Christmas Navidad (*f.*)
cipher cifra (*f.*)
circle círculo (*m.*)
circulatory system aparato
  (*m.*) circulatorio
circumference circunferencia
  (*f.*)
citizenship conducta (*f.*)

city ciudad (*f.*)
civil civil
class clase (*f.*)
classmate compañero(-a)
  de clase
clean limpiar, limpio(-a)
cleanliness limpieza (*f.*)
clear claro(-a)
climate clima (*m.*)
close cerrar (e:ie), cerca (de)
closet ropero (*m.*)
clothes ropa (*f.*)
coagulate coagular
coast costa (*f.*)
coat abrigo (*m.*)
cockroach cucaracha (*f.*)
cold frío(-a)
colon dos puntos
colonize colonizar
colony colonia (*f.*)
color color (*m.*), pintar,
  colorear
combination combinación (*f.*)
come venir
come back regresar, volver
  (o:ue)
comma coma (*f.*)
common común
  —**noun** nombre (*m.*),
    (sustantivo) (*m.*) común
communism comunismo (*m.*)
compass compás (*m.*)
compose componer
composition composición (*f.*)
compound compuesto(-a)
comprehension comprensión
concept concepto (*m.*)
condensation condensación (*f.*)
conduct conducta (*f.*)
cone cono (*m.*)
congress congreso (*m.*)
congressman representante
congresswoman representante
conjunction conjunción (*f.*)
conquer conquistar
conqueror conquistador
consonant consonante (*f.*)
constellation constelación (*f.*)
constitution constitución (*f.*)
construction paper cartulina
  (*f.*)
consume consumir
contest concurso (*m.*)
continent continente (*m.*)
continue continuar
contraction contracción (*f.*)
conversation conversación (*f.*)

cooperation cooperación (*f.*)
copy copiar, copia (*f.*)
corner esquina (*f.*)
corpuscle glóbulo (*m.*)
correct correcto(-a), bien,
  corregir (e:i)
cotton algodón (*m.*)
count contar (o:ue)
country país (*m.*)
cover cubrir
covered (with)
  cubierto(-a) (de)
cow vaca
crab cangrejo (*m.*)
crocodile cocodrilo (*m.*)
cry llorar
cubic cúbico(-a)
cup taza (*f.*)
cure curar, cura (*f.*)
curved curvo(-a)
cut cortar, recortar
cyclone ciclón (*m.*)
cylinder cilindro (*m.*)

D

Dad papá
daisy margarita (*f.*)
dark oscuro(-a)
date fecha (*f.*), fechar
daughter hija
day día (*m.*)
de of, from, about
  —**visita** visiting
decade década (*f.*)
decimal decimal
decimeter decímetro (*m.*)
declare declarar
decrease disminuir
defeat vencer
definite definido(-a)
  —**article** artículo (*m.*)
    definido
definition definición (*f.*)
degree grado (*m.*), título (*m.*)
democracy democracia (*f.*)
denary decena (*f.*)
denominator denominador
  (*m.*)
depend depender
depression depresión (*f.*)
desert desierto (*m.*)
desk escritorio (*m.*)
diameter diámetro (*m.*)
dictation dictado (*m.*)
dictionary diccionario (*m.*)
diet dieta (*f.*)
difference diferencia (*f.*)

different diferente, distinto(-a)
digest digerir (e:ie)
digestion digestión (*f.*)
digestive digestivo(-a)
—**system** aparato (*m.*) digestivo
diminish disminuir
director director(-a)
discover descubrir
disease enfermedad (*f.*)
dissolve disolver (o:ue)
divide dividir
dividend dividendo (*m.*)
divisible divisible
division división (*f.*)
divisor divisor (*m.*)
do hacer
dog perro(-a)
doll muñeca (*f.*)
domestic doméstico(-a)
door puerta (*f.*)
dotted line línea (*f.*) de puntos
double doble
down abajo
draw dibujar, trazar (*i.e. a line*)
drawer cajón (*m.*), gaveta (*f.*)
drawing dibujo (*m.*)
drill práctica (*f.*)
drink beber, tomar
drizzle lloviznar, llovizna (*f.*)
duck pato(-a)
during durante

E

each cada
earth tierra (*f.*)
earthquake terremoto (*m.*)
East este (*m.*)
easy fácil
eat comer
effort esfuerzo (*m.*)
egg huevo (*m.*)
elbow codo (*m.*)
elect elegir (e:i), escoger
election elección (*f.*)
electricity electricidad (*f.*)
electron electrón
element elemento (*m.*)
elephant elefante (*m.*)
empty vacío(-a)
energy energía (*f.*)
England Inglaterra
enroll matricular(se)
enter entrar (en)
envelope sobre (*m.*)
equilateral equilátero
equivalence equivalencia (*f.*)

erase borrar
eraser borrador (*m.*)
esophagus esófago (*m.*)
essential esencial
establish establecer
established establecido(-a)
Europe Europa
even (*number*) par
event acontecimiento (*m.*), suceso (*m.*)
evaporation evaporación (*f.*)
everybody todos(-as), todo el mundo
exact exacto(-a)
exactly exactamente
exam examen (*m.*)
example ejemplo (*m.*)
exclamation mark signo (*m.*) de admiración
excellent excelente
except excepto
exception excepción (*f.*)
exercise ejercicio (*m.*)
exist existir
expensive caro(-a)
explain explicar
eye ojo (*m.*)
eyeglasses anteojos (*m.*), gafas (*f.*), lentes (*m.*), espejuelos (*m.*)

F

face cara (*f.*)
factor factor (*m.*)
farmland tierra (*f.*) cultivable
fast rápido (-a)
fasten abrochar
fat grasa (*f.*), gordo(-a)
father padre, papá
feather pluma (*f.*)
feed alimentar, dar de comer
felt fieltro (*m.*)
field campo (*m.*)
—**trip** excursión (*f.*)
fight pelear(se), pelea (*f.*)
figure figura (*f.*)
fill out llenar
filter filtrar, filtro (*m.*)
final final
find encontrar (o:ue), hallar
finger dedo (*m.*)
finish terminar, acabar
finished terminado(-a), acabado(-a)
fire fuego (*m.*), incendio (*m.*)
first primero (-a)
fishing pesca (*f.*)

flag bandera (*f.*)
floor piso (*m.*), suelo (*m.*)
flower flor (*f.*)
fly mosca (*f.*), volar (o:ue)
food alimento (*m.*), comida (*f.*)
foot pie (*m.*)
fold doblar
folded doblado(a-)
for para, por
forget olvidar(se) (de)
form forma (*f.*), planilla (*f.*), formar
formula fórmula (*f.*)
found fundar
fourth cuarto(-a)
fowl ave (*f.*)
fraction quebrado (*m.*), fracción (*f.*) común
frame armazón (*f.*), marco (*m.*)
France Francia
free libre, gratis
front frente (*m.*)
funny gracioso(-a), cómico(-a)
future futuro(-a), futuro (*m.*)

G

gallon galón (*m.*)
garden jardín (*m.*)
garlic ajo (*m.*)
gaseous gaseoso (-a)
general general
generally generalmente
geography geografía (*f.*)
geometry geometría
germ microbio (*m.*)
get conseguir (e:i)
—**angry** enojarse
—**fat** engordar
—**hurt** lastimarse
—**nourishment** alimentarse
—**off** bajar(se)
—**on** subir(se)
—**ready** prepararse
giraffe jirafa (*f.*)
girl chica, muchacha, niña
give dar, regalar
—**back** devolver (o:ue)
gladiolus gladiolo (*m.*)
globe globo (*m.*) terráqueo
glue pegar, goma (*f.*) de pegar
go ir
—**by** pasar
—**down** bajar, disminuir
—**up** subir, aumentar
goat cabra (*f.*)

govern gobernar
government gobierno (*m.*)
governor gobernador(-a)
grade grado (*m.*)
gram gramo (*m.*)
grape uva (*f.*)
grapefruit toronja (*f.*)
    pomelo (*m.*)
gray gris
greet saludar
greeting saludo (*m.*)
group grupo (*m.*)
grow crecer
growing crecimiento (*m.*)
guess adivinar
gulf golfo (*m.*)

H

habit hábito (*m.*)
hair pelo (*m.*), cabello (*m.*)
half mitad (*f.*), medio (a)
hand mano (*f.*)
handwriting letra (*f.*)
happen pasar, ocurrir, suceder
happy feliz, contento(-a)
have tener
    —**lunch** almorzar (o:ue)
head cabeza (*f.*)
health salud (*f.*)
heart corazón (*m.*)
heat calor (*m.*)
height altura (*f.*), estatura (*f.*)
help ayuda (*f.*), ayudar
hen gallina (*f.*)
here aquí, acá
hexagon hexágono (*m.*)
high alto(-a)
hippopotamus hipopótamo
    (*m.*)
history historia (*f.*)
hit pegar, golpear
hold coger, tomar, sostener
    —**hands** tomarse de las
    manos
Holland Holanda
home hogar (*m.*), en casa
homework tarea (*f.*)
horizontal horizontal
horse caballo (*m.*)
hot cálido(-a), caliente
hour hora (*f.*)
how cómo
    —**many** cuántos (-as)
hundred cien, ciento(-a),
    centena (*f.*)
hundredth centésima (*f.*)

hurricane huracán (*m.*)
hurry up apurarse, darse prisa
hurt lastimar(se)
hydrogen hidrógeno (*m.*)
hygiene higiene (*f.*)
hyphen guión (*m.*)

I

if si
ill enfermo(-a)
illustration ilustración (*f.*),
    lámina (*f.*)
imagination imaginación (*f.*)
improper fraction quebrado
    (*m.*) impropio, fracción
    (*f.*) impropia
improve mejorar
in en, dentro (de)
    —**fact** en realidad
    —**front of** delante de
inch pulgada (*f.*)
inclined inclinado(-a)
    —**plane** plano (*m.*) inclinado
include incluir
included incluido(-a)
increase aumentar
indefinite indefinido(-a)
    —**article** artículo (*m.*)
    indefinido
independence independencia
    (*f.*)
independent independiente
Indian indio(-a)
industry industria (*f.*)
inexpensive barato(-a)
inhabitant habitante (*m.*)
inner ear oído (*m.*)
inorganic inorgánico(-a)
inside dentro, adentro
insect insecto (*m.*)
instruction instrucción (*f.*)
intelligent inteligente
interjection interjección (*f.*)
intestine intestino (*m.*)
invertebrate invertebrado (*m.*)
iron hierro (*m.*)
irregular irregular
island isla (*f.*)
isosceles isósceles

J

jacket chaqueta (*f.*)
Japan Japón (*m.*)
Japanese japonés (-esa)
join unir

joint articulación (*f.*)
jump saltar
    —**rope** saltar a la cuerda

K

keep guardar, (**oneself**)
    mantener(se)
kilogram kilogramo (*m.*), kilo
    (*m.*)
kilometer kilómetro (*m.*)
kind clase (*f.*)
kindergarten jardín de infantes
    (*m.*)
kingdom reino (*m.*)
kitchen cocina (*f.*)
knee rodilla (*f.*)
know conocer, saber
knowledge conocimiento (*m.*)

L

lake lago (*m.*)
land tierra (*f.*)
language lengua (*f.*), idioma
    (*m.*)
large grande
    —**intestine** intestino grueso
    (*m.*)
larger mayor, más grande
last durar, último(-a)
late tarde
later, luego, más tarde
lathe torno (*m.*)
laugh reír(se)
law ley (*f.*)
leaf hoja (*f.*)
learn aprender
leave salir, dejar, irse
    —**alone** dejar en paz
left izquierdo(-a)
lemon limón (*m.*)
length largo (*m.*), longitud (*f.*)
let dejar, permitir
letter letra (*f.*), carta (*f.*)
lettuce lechuga (*f.*)
level nivel (*m.*)
lever palanca (*f.*)
liberate liberar
library biblioteca (*f.*)
life vida (*f.*)
light luz (*f.*), claro(a)
    —**year** año luz (*m.*)
like gustar, como
    —**this** así, de esta manera
line línea (*f.*), fila (*f.*)
    —**up** formar fila

lineal linear
　—**measures** medidas (f.) lineales, de longitud
lion león (-ona)
liquid líquido (a), líquido (m.)
　—**measure** medida (f.) de capacidad
list lista (f.)
listen escuchar
liter litro (m.)
little pequeño(-a) (size), poco(-a) (quantity)
live vivir
liver hígado (m.)
livestock ganadería (f.)
lizard lagartija (f.)
lobster langosta (f.)
located situado(-a)
long largo(-a)
　—**wave** onda larga (f.)
lose perder (e:ie)
look at mirar
　—**for** buscar
　—**out** cuidado
　—**up** buscar
low bajo(-a)
lunch almuerzo(-a)
lung pulmón (m.)

M

machine máquina (f.)
main principal
mainly principalmente
maintain mantener
maintenance mantenimiento (m.)
make hacer
　—**an appointment** pedir (e:i) turno, pedir hora
　—**an effort** esforzarse (o:ue)
　—**good use of** aprovechar
mammal mamífero (m.)
map mapa (m.)
material material (m.)
mathematics matemáticas (f.)
matter materia (f.), sustancia (f.)
maybe quizá(s), tal vez, puede ser
mayor alcalde (-sa)
mean significar
meaning significado (m.)
measure medida (f.), medir (e:i)
measurement medida (f.)
meet encontrarse (o:ue)

meridian meridiano (m.)
meter metro (m.)
metric system sistema (m.) métrico
milimeter milímetro (m.)
mile milla (f.)
milk leche (f.)
Milky Way Vía Láctea (f.)
million millón (m.)
mine mina (f.)
mineral mineral (m.)
minuend minuendo (m.)
minus menos
miss faltar(a), perder (e:ie)
mix mezclar
mixed mixto(-a)
mixture mezcla (f.)
molecule molécula (f.)
Mom mamá
monarchy monarquía (f.)
monkey mono(-a)
moon luna (f.)
mosquito mosquito (m.)
mother madre, mamá
mount monte (m.), montar
mountain montaña (f.)
mouth boca (f.)
move mover (o:ue), mudar(se)
much mucho(-a)
multiple múltiplo (m.)
multiplicand multiplicando (m.)
multiplication multiplicación (f.)
multiplier multiplicador (m.)
muscle músculo (m.)

N

name nombre (m.)
nation nación (f.), país (m.)
nature naturaleza (f.)
necessary necesario(-a)
neck cuello (m.)
needle aguja (f.)
nerve nervio (m.)
nervous nervioso(-a)
　—**system** sistema (m.) nervioso
neutral neutral
neutron neutrón (m.)
never nunca
new nuevo(-a)
next próximo(-a)
　—**to** al lado de
noise ruido (m.), barullo (m.), bulla (f.)

North norte (m.)
nose nariz (f.)
note nota (f.), notar
notebook cuaderno (m.)
noun nombre (m.), sustantivo (m.)
nourish alimentar
nourishing nutritivo(-a), alimenticio(a-)
nourishment alimento (m.)
now ahora
number número (m.), numerar
numbering system sistema (m.) de numeración
numerator numerador (m.)
nurse enfermero(-a)
nutrition nutrición (f.)

O

object complemento (m.), objeto (m.)
observe observar
obtuse obtuso
ocean océano (m.)
octagon octágono (m.)
odd impar (number), extraño(-a)
office oficina (f.)
okay bien, bueno
older mayor
on en, sobre
once una vez
　—**in a while** de vez en cuando
onion cebolla (f.)
only sólo, solamente, único(-a)
open abrir, abierto(-a)
opening abertura (f.)
operate operar
operation operación (f.)
ophthalmologist oculista (m., f.)
oral oral
　—**reading** lectura (f.) oral
orange anaranjado(-a), naranja (f.)
　—**tree** naranjo (m.)
orchid orquídea (f.)
organ órgano (m.)
organic orgánico(-a)
other otro(-a)
ounce onza (f.)
outside afuera
outstanding sobresaliente
oxygen oxígeno (m.)

P

Pacific Pacífico (m.)

padlock candado (*m.*)
page página (*f.*)
paint pintura (*f.*), pintar
painting pintura (*f.*)
pancreas páncreas (*m.*)
pansy pensamiento (*m.*)
parallel paralelo(a-),
  paralelo (*m.*)
parallelogram paralelogramo
  (*m.*)
parentheses paréntesis (*m.*)
parents padres (*m.*)
part parte (*f.*)
participate participar
participation participación (*f.*)
pass pasar
past pasado(-a), pasado (*m.*)
pattern modelo (*m.*),
  patrón (*m.*)
pay pagar
  —**attention** prestar atención
peace paz (*f.*)
pear pera (*f.*)
peek espiar
pen pluma (*f.*)
pencil lápiz (*m.*)
  —**sharpener** sacapuntas (*m.*)
peninsula península (*f.*)
pentagon pentágono (*m.*)
people gente (*f.*)
pepper pimienta (*f.*)
  —**bell** ají (*m.*)
  —**chili** chile (*m.*)
per cent por ciento
perhaps quizá(s), tal vez
perimeter perímetro (*m.*)
period punto (*m.*), período
  (*m.*)
permit permitir, dejar
perpendicular perpendicular
persecution persecución (*f.*)
person persona (*f.*)
personal personal
phosphorus fósforo (*m.*)
photograph fotografía (*f.*),
  foto (*f.*)
physical education educación
  (*f.*) física
physics física (*f.*)
pick elegir (e:i), escoger
  —**up** recoger
picture lámina (*f.*),
  cuadro (*m.*)
pie pastel (*m.*)
piece pedazo (*m.*), trozo (*m.*)
pigment pigmento (*m.*)
pilgrim peregrino(-a)

pineapple piña (*f.*)
pink rosado(-a)
pint pinta (*f.*)
pioneer pionero(-a)
plane plano (*m.*), avión (*m.*)
planet planeta (*m.*)
plant planta (*f.*)
plural plural
plus más (+)
point punto (*m.*)
pole polo (*m.*)
polygon polígono (*m.*)
population población (*f.*)
potato papa (*f.*), patata (*f.*)
pound libra (*f.*)
power potencia (*f.*), poder (*f.*)
precede preceder
preceded precedido(-a)
predicate predicado (*m.*)
prefix prefijo (*m.*)
prepare preparar(se)
preposition preposición
present presente (*m.*)
president presidente(-a)
pretty bonito(-a), lindo(-a)
prevent prevenir
prime primo
principal director(-a)
product producto (*m.*)
progress progresar, adelantar,
  progreso (*m.*)
pronounce pronunciar
proper fraction fracción (*f.*)
  propia, quebrado (*m.*) propio
property propiedad (*f.*)
prosperity prosperidad (*f.*)
protect proteger
protected protegido(-a)
protein proteína (*f.*)
proton protón (*m.*)
pulley polea (*f.*)
punish castigar
punishment castigo (*m.*)
puppet títere (*m.*)
purify purificar
puritan puritano(-a)
purple morado(-a)
push empujar
put poner
  —**away** guardar
  —**on** ponerse
  —**together** armar
puzzle rompecabezas (*m.*)
pyramid pirámide (*f.*)

Q

quantity cantidad (*f.*)

quart cuarto (*m.*)
question pregunta (*f.*)
  —**mark** signo (*m.*) de
  interrogación
quiet callado(-a)
quotation marks comillas (*f.*)
quotient cociente (*m.*)

R

rabbit conejo(-a)
radius radio (*m.*)
read leer
reading lectura (*f.*)
ready listo(-a)
reason razón (*f.*)
recess recreo (*m.*), receso (*m.*)
reciprocal recíproco(-a)
rectangle rectángulo (*m.*)
rectangular rectangular
reduce reducir
register matricular(se)
registered matriculado(-a)
regular regular
religion religión (*f.*)
religious religioso(-a)
remain quedarse
remainder residuo (*m.*)
remember recordar (o:ue),
  acordarse (o:ue) (de)
repair reparar, arreglar,
  reparación (*f.*)
report informe (*m.*)
  —**card** libreta (*f.*) de
  calificaciones
reptile reptil (*m.*)
respiratory respiratorio(-a)
  —**system** aparato (*m.*)
  respiratorio
retain retener
return regresar, volver (o:ue),
  devolver (o:ue)
review repasar, repaso (*m.*)
rhomb rombo (*m.*)
rhomboid romboide
rhyme rima (*f.*), rimar
right derecho(-a)
  —**angle** ángulo (*m.*) recto
ring sonar (o:ue), anillo (*m.*)
river río (*m.*)
Roman romano(-a)
room cuarto (*m.*),
  habitación (*f.*)
rooster gallo
root raíz (*f.*)
rope cuerda (*f.*)
rose rosa (*f.*)

rug alfombra (*f.*)
rule regla (*f.*)
ruler regla (*f.*)
run correr

S

salary sueldo (*m.*), salario (*m.*)
salivary glands glándulas (*f.*) salivales
salt sal (*f.*)
salute saludar
same mismo(-a)
sand arena (*f.*)
sandwich sándwich (*m.*)
satellite satélite (*m.*)
satisfactory satisfactorio(-a)
say decir (e:i)
saying dicho (*m.*)
scale escama (*m.*)
scalene escaleno
school escuela (*f.*), escolar
science ciencia (*f.*)
scientific científico(-a)
scissors tijera(s) (*f.*)
skeleton esqueleto (*m.*)
skin piel (*f.*)
skull cráneo (*m.*)
slave esclavo(-a)
slavery esclavitud (*f.*)
slowly despacio
sea mar (*m.*)
season estación (*f.*)
secretary secretario(-a)
seed semilla (*f.*)
segment segmento (*m.*)
semicolon punto y coma
senator senador(-a)
send enviar, mandar
sense sentido (*m.*)
   —of hearing oído
   —of smell olfato (*m.*)
   —of taste gusto (*m.*)
   —of touch tacto (*m.*)
sentence oración (*f.*)
separate separar(se)
serpent serpiente (*f.*)
several varios (-as)
sew coser
shade sombrear, sombra (*f.*)
shape forma (*f.*)
sheep oveja (*f.*)
shelf estante (*m.*)
short bajo(-a), corto(-a)
   —story cuento (*m.*)
   —wave onda (*f.*) corta
shut cerrar (e:ie)

sick enfermo(-a)
side lado (*m.*)
sight vista (*f.*)
sign signo (*m.*), firmar
silence silencio (*m.*)
silent silencioso (a), callado(-a)
simple simple
simplify simplificar
sing cantar
singular singular
sister hermana
sit sentar(se) (e:ie)
situated situado(-a)
small pequeño(-a), chico(-a)
   —intestine intestino (*m.*) delgado
   —letter minúscula (*f.*)
snail caracol (*m.*)
snake serpiente (*f.*), víbora (*f.*)
so así, así que, de manera que, de modo que
Social Sciences ciencias (*f.*) sociales
sodium sodio (*m.*)
soil tierra (*f.*)
solar solar
solid sólido(-a)
solidification solidificación (*f.*)
solution solución (*f.*)
solve resolver (o:ue)
something algo
sometimes a veces, algunas veces
son hijo
song canción (*f.*)
soon pronto
sound sonido (*m.*)
source fuente (*f.*)
South sur (*m.*)
space espacio (*m.*)
Spain España
speak hablar, platicar
speed velocidad (*f.*)
spelling ortografía (*f.*)
   —bee concurso (*m.*) de ortografía
spend pasar, gastar
sphere esfera (*f.*)
spinal cord médula (*f.*) espinal
spine columna (*f.*) vertebral
spy espiar
square cuadrado (*m.*)
   —measure medida (*f.*) cuadrada
stand, stand up pararse
star estrella

start comenzar (e:ie), empezar (e:ie)
state estado (*m.*)
stay quedarse
steal robar
stem tallo (*m.*)
step paso (*m.*), escalón (*m.*)
still todavía
stomach estómago (*m.*)
story cuento (*m.*)
straight recto(-a)
strawberry fresa (*f.*)
stress acento (*m.*)
student alumno(-a)
study estudiar, estudio (*m.*)
subject sujeto (*m.*), tema (*m.*)
subtract restar
subtraction resta (*f.*)
subtrahend sustraendo (*m.*)
suffix sufijo (*m.*)
sugar azúcar (*f.*, *m.*)
sum suma (*f.*)
sun sol (*m.*)
sunlight luz (*f.*) del sol
supervise supervisar
supervision supervisión (*f.*)
support sostener
suppose suponer
sure seguro(-a)
surname apellido (*m.*)
swallow tragar
sweet dulce, dulce (*m.*), golosina (*f.*)
swing columpio (*m.*)
syllable sílaba (*f.*)
symbol símbolo (*m.*)
synonym sinónimo (*m.*)

T

table mesa (*f.*), tabla (*f.*)
tadpole renacuajo (*m.*)
take tomar, llevar
   —a trip hacer un viaje
tall alto(-a)
teach enseñar
teacher maestro(-a)
tell decir (e:i), contar (o:ue)
telephone teléfono (*m.*)
temperate templado(-a)
tennis tenis (*m.*)
tenth décimo(-a), décima (*f.*)
territory territorio (*m.*)
thank agradecer
that que
then entonces, luego
there allí, allá

thing cosa (*f.*)
think pensar (e:ie)
thread hilo (*m.*)
throw tirar, arrojar
tiger tigre (*m.*)
time tiempo (*m.*), época (*f.*), vez (*f.*)
tissue tejido (*m.*)
today hoy
toe dedo (*m.*) del pie
tomorrow mañana
ton tonelada (*f.*)
tongue lengua (*f.*)
too también
—**much** demasiado(-a)
tooth diente (*m.*)
top arriba, de arriba
topic tema (*m.*)
total suma (*f.*), total (*m.*)
toward hacia
trace calcar
trachea tráquea (*f.*)
trash basura (*f.*)
—**can** basurero (*m.*), lata (*f.*) de la basura
tree árbol (*m.*)
triangle triángulo (*m.*)
trim recortar
trip viaje (*m.*)
true verdad, verdadero(-a)
trunk tronco (*m.*)
try tratar (de), esforzarse (o:ue) (por)
turkey pavo(-a)
turn turno (*m.*), doblar
(to be one's ____) tocarle a uno
—**into** convertirse (e:ie) (en), transformarse
—**off** apagar
turtle tortuga (*f.*)
type clase (*f.*), tipo (*m.*), escribir a máquina

U

uncle tío

under bajo, debajo de
understand comprender, entender (e:ie)
unfold desdoblar
unfortunately desgraciadamente, por desgracia
unit unidad (*f.*)
unite unir
United States Estados Unidos
until hasta
up arriba
upper de arriba
upstairs arriba
use usar, uso (*m.*)

V

vacation vacaciones (*f.*)
various varios (-as)
vegetable vegetal (*m.*)
vein vena (*f.*)
velocity velocidad (*f.*)
ventilation ventilación (*f.*)
verb verbo (*m.*)
verify comprobar (o:ue)
vertebrate vertebrado (*m.*)
vertical vertical
vertix vértice (*m.*)
vice principal vicedirector(-a)
violet violeta (*f.*)
visit visitar
visiting de visita
vitamin vitamina (*f.*)
vocabulary vocabulario (*m.*)
volunteer voluntario(-a)
vowel vocal (*f.*)

W

wait esperar
walk caminar
war guerra (*f.*)
warm cálido(-a)
watch vigilar, reloj (*m.*)
water agua (*f.*)
—**color** acuarela (*f.*)
weak débil

wealth riqueza (*f.*)
weight peso (*m.*)
—**measure** medida (*f.*) de peso
well bien
West oeste (*m.*)
what qué, cuál, lo que
when cuándo
where dónde
which cuál (es)
white blanco(-a)
—**corpuscles** glóbulos blancos
who quién, quiénes
whole entero (*m.*)
whose de quién
why? ¿por qué?
width ancho (*m.*)
wild salvaje, silvestre
window ventana (*f.*)
windpipe tráquea (*f.*)
with con
without sin
—**fail** sin falta
word palabra (*f.*)
work trabajo (*m.*), trabajar
world mundo (*m.*), mundial
wow! ¡uy!
write escribir
wrong mal, equivocado(-a)

Y

yard yarda (*f.*) (*meas.*), patio (*m.*)
yarn estambre (*m.*), lana (*f.*) de tejer
year año (*m.*)
yellow amarillo(-a)
yet todavía
younger menor, más joven

Z

zebra cebra (*f.*)
zoo zoológico (*m.*)
zoology zoología (*f.*)